D1452719

THRICE-BORN

THRICE-BORN

THE RHETORICAL COMEBACK OF JIMMY SWAGGART

Michael J. Giuliano

MERCER UNIVERSITY PRESS
1979 - 1999
TWENTY YEARS OF PUBLISHING EXCELLENCE

ISBN 0-86554-633-9   MUP/H473

Library of Congress Cataloging-in-Publication Data
Additional Information to be Provided

Giuliano, Michael James, 1959-
    Thrice-Born: The rhetorical comeback of Jimmy Swaggart/ by
Michael J. Giuliano
    pp.   cm.
Includes bibliographical references and index.
ISBN 0-86554-633-9 (alk. paper).
1. Swaggart, Jimmy. 2. Rhetoric—Religious aspects—Christianity.
I. Title.
BC3785.S84G58   1999
269'.2'092—dc21
[B]   99-22832
                                                      CIP

CONTENTS

PREFACE

I remember it clearly. On a frigid day in February, 1988, I sat on the edge of the bed in the Super Eight Motel in Oshkosh, Wisconsin. As usual, the members of my debate team were late, so I sat channel surfing through the Sunday morning television offerings. On one of the stations, a vaguely familiar face filled up most of the screen. It was that televangelist Jimmy Swaggart, the one who I had heard was in a bit of trouble. I had watched his program a few times before, but I had never seen anything quite like this. Swaggart, with a broken voice and a tear-stained face, pleaded for forgiveness from just about everyone in his acquaintance. I was at once touched and intrigued. That intrigue led to a little extra research, which eventually led to an obsession, which culminated in a doctoral dissertation, and now a book.

What caught my attention in the months just after that televised sermon was the speed with which Swaggart recaptured his audience. While most media observers were predicting that the scandal would ruin Swaggart forever, the once king of religious television methodically went about the business of damage control. And he was soon successful in stemming the tide of defections from the Swaggart mystique. But outside observers did not seem to completely grasp how he accomplished this feat. Of course, neither did I at first. But the more I read and the more I studied, the more I realized that Swaggart had successfully woven theological doctrines and well-known narratives into a covert yet compelling defense of his character.

Most books or articles that deal with Swaggart since 1988 speak of him as a tragic failure. This book is a story of success. This is a story of one man's rhetorical campaign to recapture as much of his fame and finances as he possibly could, given the fact that the world now knew that he was a regular friend of pornography and prostitutes.

I am grateful to many people whose help and inspiration pushed me to complete this project. To my wife, Barbara, thank you for constantly reminding me how good it will feel when this book is finished. To my three children, Josh, Justin, and Linnae, thanks for understanding why Dad had to be gone just a few extra nights and weekends. To my initial dissertation committee, Dr. Irving Rein, Dr. Franklyn Haiman, and Dr. Michael Leff of Northwestern University, thank for your straightforward input into the dissertation, which now grows up into a book. To my tireless secretaries, Laura Wilson and Janet Kramer, thanks for the constant proofreads and retypes. To my two Westmont College student assistants, Stephanie Freemon and Sarah Fawcett, thanks for checking and rechecking all of those endnotes. And to my editor, Andrew Manis and all of the staff at Mercer University Press, thanks for seeing the present potential in a project about a past event.

1

THE PLAN:
A STRATEGIC RESURRECTION

If you can be born twice, why not a third time?

—Sociologist Todd Gitlin[1]

ON FEBRUARY 21, 1988, TELEVANGELIST JIMMY LEE SWAGGART launched his attempt at a third birth by delivering what *Time* magazine would label "without question, the most dramatic sermon ever aired on television."[2] With an audience of over 8,000 people jammed into the Family Worship Center of Baton Rouge, Louisiana, and one week later, with an estimated 100 million viewers worldwide looking on via television,[3] Swaggart delivered a tear-filled apology for his indiscretions with a New Orleans prostitute. News of his ignominy reached the press just three days earlier, as a private investigator hired by a revenge-seeking former fellow televangelist, Marvin Gorman of Dallas, Texas successfully photographed Swaggart's rendezvous with prostitute Debra Murphree in a seedy Travel Inn motel. Gorman had lost his ministry two years earlier when Swaggart publicly accused him of numerous

---

[1]Todd Gitlin, quoted in Ray B. Browne, "The Rape of the Vulnerable," *The God Pumpers*, eds. Marshall Fishwick and Ray B. Browne (Bowling Green, OH: Bowling Green State University Popular Press, 1987), 189.

[2]Richard N. Ostling, "Now It's Jimmy's Turn," *Time* 7 March 1988: 46.

[3]A number of sources estimate that Swaggart had between 300-500 million viewers weekly. In light of the fact that most of the 3,200 stations that carried his program broadcast Swaggart three times per week, the 100 million is the estimate based upon the assumption that most regular viewers watch more than once per week. See Gregory Belanger, "Swaggart Angers Church Execs While Defending TV Empire," *New Orleans Times-Picayune*, 3 April 1988 (Newsbank SOC file 42: F1), and Mike Dunne, "Swaggart to Oversee Troubled Empire Upon Return to Pulpit," *Baton Rouge Morning Advocate* 22 May 1988 (Newsbank SOC file 53: E8).

adulterous affairs, an accusation that would ultimately led to a defamation of character lawsuit.

Much has been written about that apology sermon. But as the last words were spoken and the lights of national publicity cooled, the Swaggart rhetorical campaign to salvage his empire had just begun. In the next three months, numerous "personal" letters written to former and continuing supporters, emotional pleas from Swaggart's wife and son, and even an exorcism performed by fellow televangelist Oral Roberts on Swaggart's "demons of lust," would add to Swaggart's argument that he should be fully restored in the hearts, minds, and pocketbooks of his partisans. This campaign culminated in an equally dramatic, but much less publicized, comeback sermon which included references to a 100 feet high leviathan attacking this man of God.

Swaggart's losses as a result of his tryst were enormous. Ministry contributions and television viewership were almost immediately cut in half. But the real story of the Swaggart scandal is not that he lost almost half of his support; the real story is that he retained half of his support.

There were at least three reasons to believe that this scandal would spell the beginning of the end of the Swaggart ministries. First, the two televangelists immersed in scandal just prior to Swaggart, Jim Bakker and Oral Roberts, were led to virtual ruin by their respective transgressions. Each situation will be recounted in chapter two, but the outcome for both men was a loss of all or most of their religious television empires. Their situations led to a snowballing of public sentiment against religious television, so it seemed inevitable that Swaggart would find a similar fate.

Secondly, Swaggart's attack on scandal-ridden Bakker was widely publicized. Since he called him "a cancer that needed to be excised from the body of Christ",[4] one would think that the smell of hypocrisy would prove to be too much for Swaggart's supporters.

Finally, it seemed unlikely that Swaggart's rhetorical audience would be so forgiving inasmuch as they shared in Swaggart's Pentecostal worldview, and resulting holiness tradition. American church

---

[4]Joanne Kaufman, "The Fall of Jimmy Swaggart," *People* 7 (March 1988): 37.

historian E. Brooks Holifield explained:

> Mr. Swaggart's involvement with a prostitute is made all the more controversial by the Pentecostal and holiness tradition. The emphasis there is on external behavior as a sign of the indwelling of holiness.[5]

In other words, Swaggart's supporters were even more likely than others to be offended by his behavior as a result of their doctrinally determined lifestyle expectations.

In light of these three reasons, it is even more arresting that within months of the scandal, Swaggart would once again preach to a full church, receive over $60 million annually in donations, and be watched by over 800,000 households in this country alone.[6] This leads to the crucial question: how was Swaggart successfully able to reason that he should be fully restored? More specifically, how did Swaggart reason from Pentecostal doctrine and narrative that he was worthy of forgiveness and continued support?

In order to answer these questions, this study will focus on the rhetorical campaign that began with Swaggart's apology sermon on February 21, 1988, continued with a variety of messages sent out during his three month hiatus from public ministry, and effectively concluded with his comeback sermon on May 22, 1988.

The goals of this study are four-fold: First, through such a study one may gain greater insight into the Swaggart rhetorical campaign to salvage his empire; second, one may also gain greater insight into how other public figures could access such approaches when they are faced with scandal defenses; third, to gain greater insight into the significant world of religious broadcasting; and fourth, to expand and develop the potential uses of an important rhetorical-analytical approach, namely

---

[5]Brooks Holifield, quoted in Larry Witham, "Swaggart Differs From Other Penitents Only in Celebrity," *Washington Times*, 26 February 1988 (Newsbank SOC file 28: B9).

[6]Angela Simoneaux, "One Year Later, Swaggart Still Alive and Preaching," *Baton Rouge Morning Advocate*, 19 February 1988 (Newsbank SOC file 22: F1).

Stephen Toulmin's model of informal argument.

The value of such a study begins with the need to understand the world of religious broadcasting. With over 1600 television ministers[7] reaching 500 million viewers weekly,[8] who contribute an estimated $2 billion annually,[9] the size and scope of this rhetorical activity is indeed notable. Moreover, despite what some media personnel suggest,[10] televangelism has continued to flourish since the scandals, and there is every reason to believe that it will continue to do so. As rhetorical critic Quentin Schultze argues throughout his book, *Televangelism and American Culture*, televangelism is a logical expression of deep-seated American cultural norms and values. Thus scandalous behavior alone is unlikely to have caused the downfall of this rhetorical activity. Indeed, since the scandals, a number of new figures on the scene, particularly Benny Hinn and Dwight Thompson, have enjoyed phenomenal success in crusade attendance and television viewership. It seems that the public may demand a change of players following a scandal, but the game continues to thrive.

Before the scandal, Swaggart was the most significant of all the religious broadcasters. In 1987, Swaggart received direct contributions of $150 million and an estimated worldwide viewership of 100 million on 3,200 stations in 143 countries.[11] As pointed out by many in the press, his success was due in no small part to his rhetorical prowess. ABC's Ted Koppel called Swaggart "a master of communication;"[12] "a man of enormous telegenuity."[13] CBS's Dan Rather referred to

---

[7]"The Koppel Report: Televangelism," narrated by Ted Koppel, produced by Lionel Chapman, directed by Jan Rifkinson, ABC, 26 February 1988.

[8]Michael Horton, preface, *The Agony of Deceit*, ed. Michael Horton (Chicago: Moody, 1990), 12.

[9]Richard Ostling, "TV's Unholy Row," *Time,* 6 April 1987, 60.

[10]Koppel argued in "The Koppel Report" that the support base for televangelism was dwindling, and would probably continue to do so. See also Quentin Schultze, *Televangelism and American Culture* (Grand Rapids: Baker, 1991), 247.

[11]Belanger (Newsbank: F1).

[12]"Crisis in Baton Rouge," narrated by Ted Koppel, *Nightline,* American Broadcasting Corporation, 22 February 1988.

[13]"The Koppel Report."

Swaggart as "the most effective speaker in the country."[14] Schultze described the apology sermon as "the single most effective televisual performance of any American evangelist."[15] Indeed, to study Swaggart's rhetoric is to study a man adept at using the spoken word to change hearts and minds.

Of course, Swaggart is not the only public figure to feel the heat of public scrutiny concerning an accusation of wrongdoing. Many cultural critics have observed our public obsession with scandal. From Presidents to major league ball players, rarely a month goes by without the hint of evil by one of our public icons. Although the particular audiences that a public figure must appease will change, I suspect that we will find that the communication strategies of public figures who successfully defend themselves from the snare of scandal tend to be strikingly similar. An analysis of Swaggart's situation will aid us in our attempt to make sense out of other scandal narratives.

Finally, I hope this study will enhance our understanding of the potential and utility of a particular method of evaluation—namely Stephen Toulmin's paradigm of informal argument. Scholars typically employ Toulmin's concepts when when the existence of an argument is obvious. But in the Swaggart campaign to salvage his empire, the link between purpose, claim, and data were often very subtle. This was especially common in Swaggart's use of Pentecostal doctrine and narratives, the two areas of concentration for this study. We will find that Toulmin's practical argument paradigm may be insightfully applied to many different types of discourse.

WHY DOCTRINE, NARRATIVE, AND TOULMIN?

The selection of methodology in rhetorical criticism should result from the answers to three questions: (1) What is the goal of rhetorical criticism in general? (2) What critical impulse draws the critic to this particular text? i.e. What is it about this particular discourse that carries

---

[14]Dan Rather, *Current Biography* (October 87): 51.
[15]Schultze, *Televangelism*, 104.

interesting critical potential? (3) What critical approaches are suggested by the nature of this specific rhetorical text and context?

In terms of the overall goal of rhetorical criticism, Edwin Black's classic work *Rhetorical Criticism: A Study in Method* still provides the most lucid explanation of the primary goal of the critic of rhetorical discourse. Black compares the task of the critic to that of the scientist:

> Yet, the critic is not so different from the scientist as one might suppose. Both have in common two vitally important activities, which are to see a thing clearly and to record what they have seen precisely.[16]

Black further posits that criticism is a "discipline that, through the investigation and appraisal of the activities and products of men, seeks as its end the understanding of man himself."[17] Thus, critical methodology is likely to illuminate how and why the discourse worked the way it did, and what that reveals about the human condition.

Secondly, the critic must consider the particular impulse that draws him or her to this particular rhetor (speaker, one who uses rhetoric) and this particular discourse. The real story behind the Swaggart scandal is not that he lost almost fifty percent of his following, but that he *retained* over half of it. In light of the outcomes of previous scandalous televangelists, in light of Swaggart's pre-scandal comments, and in light of the Pentecostal holiness tradition, the more important question is, how was Swaggart able to reason convincingly that he should be fully restored?

Lastly, particular rhetorical contexts and particular critical texts will suggest particular critical approaches. In this case, the rhetorical situation and the text reveal that to understand this discourse, this rhetor, and these auditors, we must pay careful attention to Swaggart's use of Pentecostal doctrine and his use of narrative in his scandal

---

[16]Edwin Black, *Rhetorical Criticism: A Study in Method* (Madison: University of Wisconsin Press, 1965), 4.
[17]Ibid., 9.

defense.

Both in proclamation and in practice, Swaggart and his primary audience are a doctrinally-centered community. The Assemblies of God denomination, of which Swaggart was the leading member before the scandal, begins its articles of faith with "The Bible is the Infallible Word of God."[18] Swaggart expands on this in the statement of faith section of his monthly magazine, *The Evangelist*. On page one of every issue, the first doctrinal axiom proclaims, "We believe the Bible is the inspired and only infallible and authoritative written Word of God."[19] Swaggart explicates even further in his book *Straight Answers to Tough Questions*:

> As a Christian, you *must* [emphasis his] get into the Word for yourself—study it, prove it, and allow it to be anchored to your heart. The Scriptures exhort us to "meditate therein day and night." It is critical that Christians steer clear of error and remain grounded in the truth of God's Word, always bearing good fruit. So, there is such a thing as false doctrine and there is such a thing as sound doctrine. Sound doctrine is simply what is preached and practiced according to the Word of God by preachers and teachers who have rightly divided the Word of Truth. For a doctrine to be true, it must be compatible with all the Bible—from Genesis to Revelation. If it is true doctrine, it will be taught consistently throughout Scripture. It will not leave questions unanswered or Scriptures unexplained.[20]

Content analysis also confirms that doctrine plays a key role. Every one of Swaggart's messages begins with the reading of a Bible passage, and most of the sermons include an additional five to twenty references

---

[18]Thomas F. Zimmerman, "Priorities and Beliefs of Pentecostals," *Christianity Today* 4 (September 1981): 36.

[19]"We Believe," *The Evangelist* (April 1988): 3.

[20]Jimmy Swaggart, *Straight Answers to Tough Questions* (Brentwood: Wolgemuth, 1987), 3-5.

to the Bible.[21] For Swaggart and his audience, everything that is true must be confirmed, or at least compatible with, the teachings of the Bible.

Rhetorical critic Roderick Hart has expanded our understanding of doctrinally-centered communities in his consideration of the relationship between doctrinal dogmatism and rhetorical choices. He posits that doctrinal groups can be rhetorically defined as possessing four common characteristics:

> (1) Indoctrinated listeners are counted on to make rhetorical contributions; (2) Doctrine defines the intellectual resources used by its spokespersons; (3) Doctrine defines the rhetorical role of the speakers; (4) Doctrine defines the nature of the rhetorical relationship or bond maintained between doctrinal spokesmen and their listeners.[22]

Clearly, Swaggart and his primary audience demonstrate these characteristics. In terms of the first characteristic, Hart is simply saying, in Toulmin's terms, that indoctrinated audiences fill in unspoken warrants from their reservoir of shared doctrinal beliefs. The second characteristic is a result of the creed explained in the above quote from *Straight Answers to Tough Questions*. It is not always mandatory, as we shall see later on, that everything Swaggart says is backed up by a biblical text, but it is mandatory that Swaggart say nothing that is contradicted by a biblical teaching, as understood by his audience.

Swaggart and his audience also demonstrate characteristics three and four in how they see his role in their rhetorical exchange. Swaggart is referred to as "the anointed," and the man "called by God." Swaggart himself proclaims "I am called of God: I must preach what I feel the Lord gives me to preach, as with [the Apostle] Paul, there is a divine

---

[21]David E. Davis, *A Structural Analysis of Four Religious Programs: The Effect of Program Structure on Ethos* (Educational Resources Information Center, 1984), 26. Also, personal observation of twenty Swaggart television programs have confirmed this.

[22]Roderick P. Hart, "The Rhetoric of the True Believer," *Speech Monographs* 4 (November 1971): 251.

calling upon my life."[23] This doctrinally derived understanding of role and relationship makes it very clear what Swaggart can say and do, and how he can go about it.

To understand the rhetoric of Jimmy Swaggart, one must understand the doctrinal beliefs he shares with his primary audience. But in the particular rhetoric we are examining, it is Swaggart's character that is in question, and many of the doctrinal presuppositions of the Pentecostal world view are not overtly intended to serve as character defense. It is therefore not enough that we merely understand what Pentecostals believe; we must also understand how what they believe can be transformed to serve as a character witness. Swaggart was even able to use acts that would seem to serve no ethos-building purpose—such as "glossolalia," or speaking in tongues, to make a case for continued support.

Narrative is the second key to understanding the Swaggart rhetorical campaign. Swaggart was and is a consistent storyteller. This is not surprising, considering the fact that Swaggart is a *religious* rhetor, a *southern* rhetor, and a *television* rhetor. Since Swaggart is committed to a biblical worldview, it is to be expected that he would make use of storytelling. Much of the Bible is cast in narrative form, and the Bible serves as Swaggart's primary proof text. Beyond his religious orientation, however, Swaggart is a southern rhetor, with his congregation, college, and much of his television audience sharing in that regional affiliation. Rhetorical critic Quentin Schultze pointed out the effect of southern culture on the style of the region's ministers and ministries: "Southern churches continue to be more directly influenced by the region's oral culture, which puts more emphasis on storytelling, vernacular, and especially on the power of the speaker to engage an audience."[24]

Perhaps most importantly, Swaggart is a televangelist, a profession that, due to its communication medium, demands a style geared toward entertainment and simple story lines. Schultze explains:

---

[23]Swaggart, *Straight Answers,* 150.
[24]Schultze, *Televangelism,* 84.

American evangelicalism follows a dramatic trail on television. . . . The medium's insatiable appetite for action and
emotion has profoundly affected how it communicates religious
faith. Televangelism and popularized commercial television
increasingly share this moralistic sense of drama. On Sunday-
morning television, just as during prime time, it is almost
always clear who are the good guys and bad guys. Televangelists increasingly specialize in creating unambiguously evil
characters, groups, and movements for their viewers. If
someone is evil he is heretical, immoral, liberal, and so forth.
The specific litanies of evil change from year to year, largely
with the news.[25]

Clearly, if we are to understand Swaggart and his rhetoric, we must, as
Michael McGee and John Nelson put it, understand "how reason, story,
and community relate."[26]

But as in the case of doctrine, we are interested not simply in which
narratives are told, but how narratives can function in Swaggart's
attempt at gaining forgiveness and restoration. Some of the stories
Swaggart told during his rhetorical campaign obviously affected his
goal of ethos-building. Some of the stories, however, did not overtly
argue for any particular conclusion. That is why it is necessary to pay
significant attention to the links between story and the goal of restoration. The best methodological lens to use in order to view such a link
is Stephen Toulmin's paradigm of informal argument.

Philosopher Stephen Toulmin has developed one of the best known
methods for describing and analyzing informal logic. Hart explains:

Toulmin's approach was a reaction to the models of formal
logic then popular in philosophical circles. He felt that such
models were too static to deal with something as dynamic as

---

[25]Schultze, *Televangelism*, 98, 102, 117.
[26]Michael Calvin McGee and John S. Nelson, "Narrative Reason in Public
Argument," *Journal of Communication* 35 (Autumn 1985): 139.

human thought and so he proposed a system better adapted to the actual logic used by actual people. Toulmin did not prescribe how people ought to reason; instead, he tried to describe how they actually behaved.[27]

Thus, Toulmin's concern is how an argument works for a particular auditor or group of auditors, not how it works in fulfillment of some formal criteria of logical validity.

The core of Toulmin's analysis is his layout of practical argument. Toulmin argues that all arguments have at least three components: claims, data (or grounds, as he is presently calling them), and warrants. The claim answers the question "What are you trying to prove?" It is the conclusion, the idea one wants an audience to accept. For example, a person may say, "You should cut down on your consumption of red meat." The statement is a claim, and may be accepted on its face, but most claims need support, or data, if it is likely to be accepted. Data consist of the materials used by to convince an auditor that one's claim is sound. In this example, the arguer may say, "red meat is bad for your health—the Surgeon General said so." Again, this support may be sufficient for acceptance, but in almost all situations, a convincing argument must include one final component—a "warrant." A warrant is the bridge between data and claim. A warrant answers the question, "Why should the data convince me of the claim?" In this case, the answer would be, "The surgeon general is a reliable source who speaks based upon reliable information." Obviously, warrants are often unstated, and mentally contributed by the auditor to complete the argument.

I suggest two reasons for using Toulmin's methodology and terminology for evaluating Swaggart's rhetoric of apology. First, these terms emphasize the existence of credibility-enhancing arguments in doctrines and narratives that often do not initially appear to argue for such a claim. Second, this emphasis on warrants leads the outsider into the shared worldview of rhetor and auditor. Swaggart's warrants were

---

[27]Hart, *Modern Rhetorical Criticism* (Glenview Scott, 1990), 138-139.

virtually always unstated, but their acceptance by his audience completed the argument. Even in narratives, shared assumptions about the world link those stories to the claim that Swaggart was worthy of continued support. Toulmin's emphasis on warrants best accounts for the hidden reasons for Swaggart's rhetorical success. As we will see, success was no stranger to Swaggart. His communication skills had served him well, long before the crucial events of 1988.

2

THE SPEAKER:
THE LIFE & TIMES OF A
PROTESTANT POPE

Welcome to Ferriday, Louisiana: Home of Mickey Gilley, Jerry Lee Lewis, Jimmy Swaggart, and Mrs. U. B. Evans, Nationally Known Horticulturist.

—Billboard on the road into Ferriday, Louisiana

ALTHOUGH THE LINEAGE OF MRS. EVANS IS UNKNOWN, IT IS CERTAIN that at least the first three favorite sons of Ferriday are all members of the same family. Swaggart's memories of his two iconic cousins are found on many of the pages of his autobiography. In fact, after describing his birth in 1935 and his family's early days, which found them so poor that "practically every member of the family—plus an assortment of other relatives—went into bootlegging whiskey just to make enough money to survive,"[1] Swaggart cast most of the remaining pages of his personal narrative as a comparison between Jerry Lee's rise to fame and his own rise to television stardom.

Virtually all we know about Swaggart's early years is found within the pages of his autobiography. Swaggart recounts the forces that shaped his destiny as the result of three visions he received, two of which occurred when he was a child. The first one appeared when he was eight. Jerry Lee, Mickey, and Jimmy made a regular pilgrimage to the Arcade movie theater every Saturday. On one particular Saturday, however, Swaggart was alone. As he stood in line to get his ticket,

---

[1]Jimmy Swaggart, *To Cross A River* (Baton Rouge: Jimmy Swaggart Ministries, 1984), 11.

suddenly he heard an "entreating" voice proclaim: "Do not go in this place. Give your heart to me. I have chosen you as a vessel to be used in my service." Wanting so much to see the movie, Jimmy ignored the voice as a figment of his imagination. When the voice repeated the call, however, Swaggart gave in: "The words were so strong chill bumps broke out on my arm. My hair tingled. Somehow the words had so much power, I couldn't resist them. I had to yield."[2] Swaggart would retell this story often, referring to it as his conversion or salvation experience. It was also this notion of a call to God's service that would define Swaggart's role in the future.

Swaggart's second divine message would take place one year later in the summer of 1944. One day, as Jimmy and Jerry Lee lazily played in the Louisiana sun, Swaggart had a jolting experience:

> The first time the Lord spoke through me prophetically I didn't know what was happening. I felt like I was standing outside my body. Then I began to describe exactly what I saw . . . a powerful bomb destroying an entire city . . . tall buildings crumbling . . . people screaming.[3]

According to Swaggart, God caused him to give these prophesies in unknown languages, or tongues. He remembered that war veterans who were present at the time of the prophecies told him he had spoken in Japanese and German. But despite this evidence of the miraculous, Swaggart recalls that he was loudly criticized and ridiculed for such proclamations. Predictably, criticism of his prophetic ability ceased the day that the bombs were dropped on Japan.

Interestingly, Swaggart de-emphasized this notion of receiving specific prophecies from God once he rose to ministry prominence. This narrative, however, serves to reinforce Swaggart's contention that God called him not only to serve, but to serve in unique and mighty ways. It was fourteen years later before Swaggart heard from God

---

[2]Swaggart, *To Cross*, 21-22.
[3]Swaggart, *To Cross*, 44-45.

again. By 1958, Swaggart had married Frances Anderson, had dropped out of high school, and had began to hold evangelistic meetings in small towns across Louisiana. As he grieved over his family's dire poverty, and as he considered his cousin Jerry Lee's massive wealth and fame, he began to reconsider the wisdom of his decision to enter into God's service. Chapple summarizes Swaggart's experience:

> On the fourth night of a revival in 1958, Jimmy Lee took sick with pneumonia. Had he chosen the wrong road? Jerry Lee was driving Cadillacs. Cousin Mickey had smartened up too. Voices spoke to Jimmy Lee on his sickbed: "Your God cannot heal you." Jimmy Lee cried out and picked up the Bible. Joshua 1:9: "Be not afraid, neither by thou dismayed: for the Lord thy God is with thee whithersoever thou goest." Jimmy Lee had been sick long enough. "Elvis Presley can have *Hound Dog* . . . Jerry Lee can have *Great Balls of Fire*, but I'll take the Holy Ghost and fire. Hallelujah!"[4]

According to Swaggart, after this vision, he never again doubted his decision to preach the gospel.

The 1960s witnessed the rise of Swaggart's talent and fame in two enterprises: as an itinerant preacher in the Southeast and as a recording artist. Having learned to play the piano at the side of Old Sam, an elderly African-American pianist from the south side of Ferriday, Swaggart had continued to hone his skills as a singer and musician. In 1959, he recorded his first gospel album, beginning a phenomenal string of musical successes. By 1988, he had recorded 54 albums, with a combined sale of $200 million. This achievement led the recording industry to crown him the "best-selling gospel artist in record history."[5]

Swaggart's move into the electronic media began in 1969 when he

---

[4]Steve Chapple, "Whole Lotta Savin' Goin' On," *Mother Jones,* July-August 1986: 41.

[5]Charles H. Lippy, *Twentieth-Century Shapers of American Popular Religion* (New York: Greenwood, 1989), 419.

started a weekly radio program, "The Campmeeting Hour," on stations in Atlanta, Houston, and St. Paul. In less than five years, it was one of the most popular religious broadcasts in the country.

Swaggart launched his television ministry in 1972. As he later said: "The ministry probably quadrupled with radio. With TV it exploded."[6] His weekly program quickly grew to over one hundred stations, and by 1977 he was bringing in over $600,000 a month. Such success led Swaggart to start another weekly program, "A Study in the Word." As contrasted with the fiery revival style of the "Jimmy Swaggart Hour," this program was presented in a contemplative teaching style, without a live audience.

According to the Arbitron ratings service, Swaggart had the fourth highest rated religious broadcast by 1980.[7] By 1983 Swaggart's show reached the top of the religious television charts, and stayed there until the scandal in 1988.

Triumph in the television industry inevitably brought the funds for building a physical empire. The Jimmy Swaggart Ministries built a World Ministry Center in Baton Rouge—a 257 acre complex, complete with television studio, a radio station, a 7,500 seat church auditorium, and its own zip code. In all, the complex was valued at $60 million, while the overall ministries' net worth was estimated at $142 million.

In 1984, Swaggart built the Jimmy Swaggart Bible College. In that initial year, 18,000 students applied for 400 openings.[8] The staffing needs of the college, when combined with the staff needs of the church, media, and other ministries, meant 1,200 jobs for residents of the Baton Rouge area at an annual budget of $11.5 million.

Riches for the ministry ultimately meant riches for the Swaggart family. Swaggart purchased a $2.4 million mansion that featured a four-column jacuzzi fed by a faucet shaped like a golden swan, while Swaggart's son (and assistant Pastor) Donnie, bought a $726,000

---

[6]Saundra Saperstein, "Spreading a $600,000-a-Day Message," *Washington Post*, 7 June 1987, A20.

[7]Jeffrey K. Hadden and Charles E. Swann, *Prime Time Preachers* (Reading: Addison-Wesley, 1981), 51.

[8]Ostling,"TV's Unholy Row," 63.

home. Jimmy's stated 1988 salary was $86,000, while his wife made $50,526 annually and son Donnie was paid $58,500. In addition, twenty-two Swaggart relatives were employed by the ministry, accounting for more than $350,000 of the payroll.

Swaggart also found success in the publishing industry. To date, he has written forty-two books, most of which have been regularly promoted on his television broadcasts. In addition, Swaggart's ministries put out a monthly glossy magazine—*The Evangelist.* In it, Swaggart would write at least one article, and usually more.

Another interesting aspect of Swaggart's success was his enormous popularity in Latin America. Labeled the "Protestant pope,"[9] Swaggart's programs were watched by over seventy-five percent of Central American churchgoers, and almost seventy percent of these Protestant *and* Catholic Christians felt that Swaggart's teachings were more "useful" than those of the institutional church.[10] One author theorized that Swaggart's popularity in the region could be attributed to his practice of attacking the government-supporting Catholic church, and the incredible amount of money he poured into the area by way of building churches, orphanages, and medical facilities.[11]

Prior to the sex scandal of 1988, Swaggart had been involved in two controversies of note. In 1981, the Swaggart ministries were taken to court by the family of deceased widow Zoe Vance, who had left her entire $10 million estate to Swaggart. The family claimed that ministry personnel had exploited Zoe for financial reward. They produced evidence of countless numbers of visits to the elderly woman by ministry personnel and Swaggart himself. During the trial, they also produced the log of West Coast ministry representative Ron McGregor, who labeled a 1979 visit to Zoe a "good PR call."[12] In the end,

---

[9]Schultze, *Televangelism*, 13.

[10]Dennis A. Smith, "The Gospel According to the United States," *American Evangelicals and the Mass Media*, ed. Quentin J. Schultze (Grand Rapids: Academie, 1990), 302.

[11]David Stoll, *Is Latin America Turning Protestant?* (Berkeley: University of California Press, 1990), 153.

[12]Saperstein, A20.

Swaggart received seventy percent of the estate, while the remaining funds were distributed to the immediate family members. With the court essentially ruling in Swaggart's favor, Swaggart's ministry was to feel little negative consequence from this incident.

In 1983, reporter John Camp produced a public television documentary entitled "Give Me That Big Time Religion." During the program, Swaggart was accused of five transgressions: (1) greed (2) corruption; (3) manipulation of his audiences; (4) politicizing his preaching; (5) being big-time rather than old-time religion. The most specific and serious charge was that money collected specifically for the children's aid fund were being used on ministry buildings and personal furnishings. Although no abuses were ever clearly confirmed, the ministry made changes in how monies were allocated, and the entire affair was quietly treated as an internal church matter.

SWAGGART'S RHETORICAL THEMES

Throughout his career, Swaggart's preaching has centered on three themes: (1) emphasis upon ecclesiastical separation and purity; (2) emphasis upon personal separation and purity; and (3) an emphasis upon classical Pentecostal-fundamentalist doctrines (which will be discussed in chapter four). By the time of the scandal in 1988, his primary audience had years of experience listening to these themes. Thus, fully to understand the scandal situation and its rhetoric requires an exploration of the themes his audience had grown accustomed to hearing.

Conforming to Schultze's observation that television demands simple story lines and clear delineation of good and evil, characters, etc., televangelists tend to fall into one of two categories. The quantitatively larger of these groups would be those preachers who emphasize the blessings of God available to believers in *this* life. Their theology is often referred to as the "health and wealth gospel,"[13] or the idea that God wants his children to possess physical and financial prosperity, if only they will ask him for it. This group also tends to have a very optimistic view of the potential for social, economic, and political reform, and thus they tend to be very politically active. The group of religious broadcasters who espouse a health and wealth world view have included Jim and Tammy Bakker, Kenneth Copeland, Ernest Angley, Benny Hinn, Oral Roberts, and Pat Robertson.

The second major category of preachers prefer to acknowledge the inherent difficulties of this life, while emphasizing the glory in the life to come. They tend to have a very pessimistic view of national or cultural reform and change in this world, and consequently tend to be very critical of it. Swaggart is the best known of this smaller group of religious broadcasters, and his views have led him to be the most openly critical of all the televangelists. His criticisms fall into two categories: those stemming from his emphasis on ecclesiastical purity, and those stemming from his emphasis on personal purity.

Ecclesiastical holiness refers to the idea that Christians should separate themselves from other religious entities, including other Christian groups, to maintain their purity before God. Swaggart has always been willing to battle the brethren on the airwaves, but Schultze notes that his willingness to name particular groups and people seemed to increase as his national popularity increased.[14] The following is a sampling of some of the public statements he has made concerning other religious groups.

Concerning Catholics: "A false cult" composed of "poor, pitiful individuals who think they have enriched themselves spiritually by kissing the Pope's ring."[15] On another occasion he asserted, "Mother

---

[13]See Michael Horton, "The TV Gospel," *The Agony of Deceit*, edited by Michael Horton (Chicago: Moody, 1990), 123-152; Schultze, *Televangelism*, 153-182.

[14]Schultze, *Televangelism*, 88.

[15]Stephen J. Pullum, "The Mass Appeal of Jimmy Swaggart: Pentecostal Media Star," Speech Communication Association, New Orleans, 3-6 November 1988.

Theresa is going to hell unless she gets born again."[16] Or he argued, "Catholic doctrine is literally leading millions to hell;"[17] "Most Catholics are Catholics two times a year—once at Mardi Gras and once at—I can't think of the other."[18]

Concerning mainline Protestant churches: "I hate—hate—those droning old mausoleum churches. They'd kill a dead man in a graveyard at midnight."[19] He asked his audience: "Do you realize that in most churches in America you couldn't get saved if you wanted to? Do you know that in most churches in America you can drink and adulterate and fornicate and swine and swirl and swirl and swine and still be a member in good standing?"[20] In one particular broadside, he charged that the World and National Council of Churches "work for the Devil. If you go to a church which supports these councils, get out! I'm talking about the Episcopal, United Methodists, Presbyterians, and Lutherans."[21]

Concerning Jews: "Don't bargain with Jesus: Jesus was a Jew."[22] "The extermination of the Jews was the result of their failure to believe in Jesus Christ."[23]

Concerning other televangelists: Speaking of Jim Bakker, he said, "God deliver us from these pretty little boys, with their hair done, and their nails done, calling themselves preachers of the Gospel."[24] He

---

[16]David A. Harvey, "TV Preacher Jimmy Swaggart: Why Does He Say Those Awful Things About Catholics?," *The God Pumpers*, edited by Marshall Fishwick and Ray B. Browne (Bowling Green: Bowling Green State University Popular Press, 1987), 87.

[17]Lloyd Grove, "Jimmy Swaggart's Controversial Crusade," *Washington Post,* 8 April 1987, A1.

[18]"Swaggart Reaction Varies," *Colorado Springs Gazette Telegraph*, 27 February 1988 (Newsbank SOC file 28: D13).

[19]"Swaggart Reaction Varies" (Newsbank: D13).

[20]"Swaggart Reaction Varies" (Newsbank: D13).

[21]J. D. Cardwell, *Mass Media Christianity* (Lanham: University Press of America, 1984), 105.

[22]Ostling, "TV's Unholy Row," 63.

[23]Harvey, 87.

[24]Jay Matthews, "Swaggart Undamaged by Bakker Scandal," *Washington Post,* 29 March. 1987, A4.

condemned the practices of Kenneth Copeland and Robert Schuller as the "work of the devil."[25] Speaking of Oral Roberts and Jim Bakker, he declared: "I'm ashamed, I'm embarrassed. The gospel of Jesus Christ has never sunk to such a level as it has today. We've got a dear brother in Tulsa, Oklahoma, up in a tower telling people that if they don't send money that God's going to kill him, then we got this soap opera being carried out live down in South Carolina all in the name of God."[26]

Concerning other Pentecostals: In what one pastor called the "Pentecostal Inquisition,"[27] Swaggart increased his attack on specific Pentecostal preachers and specific doctrines he thought were in opposition to fundamental Pentecostal faith. His church staff brought "doctrinal deviation" charges against one prominent Assembly of God pastor in Florida, and Swaggart has been quoted as saying that more and more Pentecostals are "engaging in false doctrines," and practicing "mental gymnastics."[28] In one sermon, he concluded that "even in our Pentecostal churches, we're forsaking the altars and the power of God and the leading and direction of the Holy Spirit and referring our people with difficulties to psychologists."[29] Concerning the public healings performed by many Pentecostal preachers and even laypersons, Swaggart proclaimed that "most of them are fake."[30]

Of course, Swaggart's attacks have not come without criticism. Not only have other religious figures gone on record as suggesting Swaggart is wrong in his attacks,[31] but the national media have often chastised Swaggart for his viciousness. Criticisms of Swaggart's aggressive style

---

[25]Lynn Rosellini, "Of Rolexes and Repentance," *U. S. News and World Report,* 7 March 1988, 63.

[26]Jeffrey K. Hadden and Anson Shupe, *Televangelism: Power and Politics on God's Frontier* (New York: Holt, 1988), 13.

[27]Grove, A8.

[28]Ibid.

[29]Pullum, "Mass Appeal," 6, 7.

[30]Lippy, 423.

[31]For example, see Richard N. Ostling, "Worshipers on a Holy Roll," *Time,* 11 April 1988, 55; James M. Wall, "Swaggart's Confession: There's Room to Mourn," *Christian Century,* 9 March 1988, 235.

have been found in *Time*,[32] *Commonweal*,[33] and *Newsweek*, which proclaimed that to Swaggart, "the Bible is a one-edged sword designed to smite any religious tradition that does not square with his own brand of Christian fundamentalism."[34]

How does Swaggart defend his practice of attacking particular persons and groups from the pulpit? He justified his actions by suggesting that the attacks are not only necessary to conduct a successful ministry, but mandatory. He argued that "It's impossible to make an omelet without breaking eggs."[35] On another occasion, he insisted, "No compromise. Today we wallow in conformity. . . . If you're wearing a blue coat and gray trousers you're gonna get shot in both sides."[36] To the question, "Why don't you preach more love instead of messages that seem sharply to criticize or condemn?" he responded, "As a minister of the Gospel, I have that same kind of obligation. The bridge is out; there is a raging torrent ahead. Certain death looms just over the horizon. Likewise, I must warn our nation; I must wake the people from their lethargy."[37]

While generally staying out of the political arena, Swaggart has never sidestepped opportunity to comment upon any of the issues he felt were at odds with the call to maintain separation from the world, or personal holiness. Such an emphasis has led him to proclaim his violent opposition to movie attendance, rock-and-roll music, pornography, drugs, alcohol, smoking, dancing (including aerobic dancing), homosexuality, abortion, divorce, and immodest clothing on women, including most forms of bathing suits. Of course, Swaggart Bible College students and all ministry personnel had to refrain from these

---

[32]Richard N. Ostling, "Power, Glory— and Politics," *Time*, 17 February 1986, 62-69.

[33]John Garvey, "Truth Flashes: What's Right About Jimmy Swaggart," *Commonweal*, 26 December 1986: 677-678.

[34]Kenneth L. Woodward, "Swaggart's One-Edged Sword," *Newsweek*, 9 January 1984, 65.

[35]Grove, A8.

[36]Grove, A8.

[37]Swaggart, *Straight Answers*, 151.

practices if they hoped to maintain their positions.

FORM AND DELIVERY IN SWAGGART'S PREACHING AND PROGRAMS

What made the Swaggart attacks even more vociferous was the powerful way in which they were delivered. Television shapes not only what is communicated, but how it is communicated. Thus, when considering the delivery of a particular television rhetor, we must consider the stylistic characteristics of both the speaker and the delivery system.

Prior to 1988, Swaggart broadcast two distinctively different programs. The less ambitious of the two is entitled "A Study in the Word." This program is shot in a studio, with Swaggart normally standing in front of a blackboard, as he takes on the pose of the careful, thoughtful teacher. Absent from this program are the theatrics and moments of extreme emotion that are the public trademarks of Swaggart's style. The topic is often biblical prophecy, and the only non-Swaggart camera shots show visual graphics enhancing whatever the subject is for that day.

Swaggart's main program is simply entitled "Jimmy Swaggart" or "The Jimmy Swaggart Broadcast." These programs are rebroadcasts of his church services, his crusade meetings, or his annual "Old Fashion Camp Meeting." The format is almost always cast in three parts. Swaggart opens up with two or three songs, sung in a style that is a cross between traditional gospel and Nashville sound. As Jeffrey Hadden and Charles Swann describe it, "Jimmy belts out good-time, hand-clapping gospel songs at the piano and sings with great feeling. He is backed up by a Nashville-style band, and even a skeptical viewer is likely to get caught up in the infectious rhythm."[38]

The vast majority of the time is devoted to Swaggart's preaching. Physically, Swaggart's delivery is best described as a vocal narrative, in which he repeatedly rises to a verbal climax. His messages are usually

---

[38]Hadden and Swann, 39.

begun in a soft-spoken voice as he introduces the Bible text for the day's sermon. Slowly, however, he begins to build to an emotional peak, both in the substantive intensity of his words and in his vocal quality. Finally, when audience and speaker have shared a moment of fever pitch, Swaggart will bring them down with his soft-spoken tones, only to begin the ride up the verbal mountain over and over again.[39] Along the way, in almost every sermon he gives,[40] he will whisper, shout, cry, wipe his brow with his handkerchief, loosen his tie, dance across the stage, and kneel on the stage. Often, he will return to the piano during his message to play one more emotion-enhancing song. In all, one has to concur with Flo Conway and Jim Siegelman's assessment of Swaggart's delivery style, which they describe as "perhaps the best instance on television of holy rolling as pure art form."[41]

The one difference between seeing Swaggart in person as opposed to seeing him on television is that his regular practice of speaking in tongues is usually edited out of the televised version. Swaggart understands that "glossolalia" is one practice many of his prospective partisans may not understand.

The final segment of the broadcast is an appeal for funds. This normally lasts no more than five minutes, and usually takes the form of an offer to buy something, such as a Swaggart book or album. This segment normally ends with an advertisement of upcoming crusades or meetings.

David E. Davis points out a number of other interesting facts in his quantitative analysis of the "Jimmy Swaggart" show. During the one

---

[39] A personal note: my strongest memory of attending the October 4, 1991 Jimmy Swaggart crusade was his ability to take his audience beyond the point of self-control. Through exquisitely crafted word images, given with the most dramatic emphasis, Swaggart's crowd was continually brought to a state of frenzy that I have never seen before. They would run around the room, dance with complete strangers, fall to the ground and shake vigorously, scream and cry, sometimes for no apparent contextual reason.

[40] I have viewed over a dozen episodes. Also, this is how he performed when I attended the crusade in San Diego. See also Pullum, "The Mass Appeal," 13.

[41] Flo Conway and Jim Siegelman, *Holy Terror* (Garden City: Doubleday, 1982), 49.

hour program, there are an average of sixty pauses for applause, and over 100 audience reaction shots. During the programs that he observed, an average of 324 camera shots were used to build the feeling of motion and excitement.[42] As Davis points out, these numbers far exceed the practices of any of the other televangelists he surveys.

Swaggart seems to understand the power of the spoken word to move audiences. To one interviewer he remarked, "I heard that Dan Rather said I was the greatest communicator in the world. That's the name of the game—communication. You've got to communicate to the people. You've got to get them to hear your message."[43] But after the scandalous events of 1988, Swaggart's ability to communicate convincing arguments was seriously put to the test.

---

[42]Davis, 15, 31, 23.

[43]Swaggart, interview with Steve Fox, *Good Morning America* ABC, WRTV, Indianapolis, 12 November 1986.

3

THE RHETORICAL SITUATION: TELEVISION'S UNHOLY ROW

I can honestly say he's genuine, and there are no skeletons in any Swaggart closet. Everything is open and above board.

—Preface to Swaggart's Autobiography[1]

He confessed to church officials that not only did he pay a prostitute to perform "pornographic" acts, but that he had an obsession with pornography since childhood.

—*Washington Post*[2]

ON FEBRUARY 18, 1988, THE MEDIA RUMOR MILL ROARED TO LIFE with the news that religious television kingpin Jimmy Swaggart had been caught consorting with a prostitute. The details would not be known for several days, but Swaggart's attempt to defuse the damage would begin in just three days, as his Sunday church and television audience would no doubt demand an explanation. The rhetorical choices he would make, however, were shaped by more than just his sexual escapades. Swaggart would have to take into account the recent misdeeds of other TV preachers, his public responses to those deeds, the media's shaping and presentation of all of the scandals, as well as the attention of additional viewers brought in by the titillation of public scandal. In short, Swaggart had to consider the entire rhetorical situation in the crafting of his defense.

---

[1]Robert Paul Lamb, preface, quoted in Swaggart, *To Cross*, vii.
[2]Laura Sessions Stepp, "The Swaggart Aftermath," *Washington Post* , 23 February 1988, D1.

Prior to Lloyd Bitzer's "rhetorical situation" perspective in 1968, communication criticism tended to view speech acts in isolation from their contexts. A speech would be analyzed for its style, arguments, and effects, quite apart from the situation that brought it into existence. Bitzer argued that all speeches are brought into existence as a response to an "exigence," defined as an "urgent problem, obstacle, something that is not as it should be."[3] With this in mind, Bitzer argued that any critic of a communication event should be vitally concerned with the "rhetorical situation." He defined the "rhetorical situation" as a "complex of persons, events, objects, and relations presenting an actual or potential exigence which can be completely or partially removed if discourse, introduced into the situation, can so constrain human decision or action as to bring about the significant modification of the exigence."[4]

Bitzer's concern was with the exploration of the circumstances that had brought the discourse into existence, the choices and limitations that the exigence presented to the speaker, and the audiences who would ultimately decide if the rhetoric was an appropriate response to the crisis. Bitzer's approach became a forceful reminder that no communication act was produced in a vacuum. If the critic was adequately to analyze any communication act, the rhetorical situation must be considered.

GODSCAM

America's year-long obsession with "TV's Unholy Row," as *Time* magazine labeled it, began in Tulsa, Oklahoma on January 4, 1987. Long-time televangelist Oral Roberts announced on his weekly program that God told him in a vision that unless he raised $4.5 million for medical missionaries by March 31, 1987, God would "take

---

[3] Karyn Rybacki and Donald Rybacki, *Communication Criticism* (Belmont: Wadsworth Publishing Co., 1991) 24.

[4] Lloyd Bitzer, "The Rhetorical Situation," *Philosophy and Rhetoric* 1 (January 1968): 1.

him home."[5] After the broadcast, Roberts immediately sent a letter to his present and former supporters. In the letter, Oral's son, Richard, pleaded, "Let's not let this be my Dad's last birthday!" while Oral recounted the message of the vision that he had received one year earlier: "I desperately need you to come into agreement with me concerning my life being extended beyond March. God said, 'I want you to use the ORU medical school to put my medical presence in the earth. I want you to get this going in one year or I will call you home.'"[6]

Controversial visions from God were not new to Roberts. He had once described a vision of a 900-foot tall Jesus who instructed him to solicit additional millions from his "partners" so that he could build his medical complex. This time, however, public criticism from secular and religious media sources exploded as never before. In fact, a number of television stations even refused to air the January 4 program. Despite this reduction in television coverage, the public was spellbound by glimpses into this sometimes seedy world of religious television, a world that many had ignored up to that point.

As it turned out, Roberts received the final $1.3 million just days before the deadline from a dog track owner in Sarasota, Florida. When asked why he did it, the philanthropist replied, "He doesn't have to commit hara-kiri now."[7] But the negative publicity dealt a blow to the Roberts's ministry from which it never fully recovered.

Swaggart seized the occasion to offer his own public criticism of Roberts. In addition to the comments mentioned earlier, Swaggart declaimed: "That would place our heavenly father . . . in the same category as a terrorist . . . . that is abominable. People who support Oral Roberts are themselves held hostage."[8] For some members of the press, this fighting between religious superpowers became more interesting and publicly marketable than the scandals themselves.

---

[5]Richard N. Ostling, "TV's Unholy Row" 60.

[6]Randy Fram, "Did Oral Roberts Go Too Far?," *Christianity Today* 20 (January 1987): 43.

[7]Ostling, "TV's Unholy Row," 67.

[8]"Swaggart Blasts Roberts for Money Demands," *Presbyterian Journal* , 4 February 1987, 63.

Before the print on the Roberts' controversy had dried, the public was treated to yet another shocking revelation concerning a religious television icon. On March 19, 1987, televangelist Jim Bakker pre-empted an expose coming out in the *Charlotte Observer* by resigning from his PTL empire. He confessed to a 1980 sexual encounter with former church secretary Jessica Hahn. But when overwhelming evidence surfaced that also suggested homosexual activity and financial aggrandizement, including a payment of $275,000 hush money to Hahn, Bakker denied any other wrongdoing. Bakker turned over his PTL (Praise the Lord) empire, which included a cable network company and a Christian theme park, to fellow televangelist Jerry Falwell. When asked why he would turn over the reins to a non-charismatic preacher, Bakker remarked that it was to stop a "diabolical takeover plot" by a rival evangelist.[9] He soon admitted that the devious devil who was after his realm was Jimmy Swaggart himself.

Swaggart denied any desire to take over PTL, but did admit that it was he who leaked the Jessica Hahn rumors to church officials.[10] Soon after that admission, Swaggart issued the public attacks upon Bakker previously mentioned. Those assaults escalated the infighting, as Roberts then maligned Swaggart for his divisiveness by asserting that "Satan has put something in your heart that you're better than anybody else."[11] Roberts would make a number of other public attacks upon Swaggart before eventually apologizing to him when Bakker was convicted of fraud in 1989.

Adding yet another chapter to televangelism's drama of 1987 and 1988 was television preacher Pat Robertson's decision to run for president. While attempting to distance himself from the title "televangelist," Robertson contributed fuel to the fire of public ridicule by claiming to receive his political orders directly from God. The derision reached its peak when Robertson accused Republican challenger, Vice

---

[9]Ostling, "TV's Unholy Row," 60.
[10]Ibid.
[11]Ostling, "TV's Unholy Row," 64.

President George Bush, of somehow orchestrating the Swaggart scandal the week before the "super Tuesday" primary vote.[12]

The demise of Roberts, Bakker, and to some extent Robertson, and the resulting attention it caused, affected Swaggart's rhetorical destiny in at least three ways. First, public opinion of televangelists reached an all-time low.[13] Even the inner-circle supporters were skeptical, as financial contributions dropped for all television preachers.[14] An increasing number of Americans were indeed interested in religious television, but not because they supported the ministries. Instead, their perceptions were being shaped by such headlines as "Godscam," "Godsgate," and "Salvationgate." If Swaggart was to be successful in his upcoming campaign, he would have to differentiate himself from the negative image that was now synonymous with the televangelism industry.

Secondly, Bakker's embarrassing failure at denial limited the probability that Swaggart could successfully use the same strategy. Added to the fact of another public figure's failure at denial—presidential candidate Gary Hart, Swaggart must have known that such a stance would not be greeted by a sympathetic public. Conversely, offering at least what appeared to be an open and honest confession would likely be well received by viewers who were tired of scoundrels who used Nixon-like repudiations in the face of overwhelming evidence.

Finally, the scandals had prompted Swaggart to make a number of public remarks regarding scandal and punishment that he would have to account for when it was his turn to defend his character. For example: "To allow a preacher of the Gospel, when he is caught beyond the shadow of a doubt committing an immoral act . . . to remain in his position as pastor, would be the most gross stupidity.[15] On another

---

[12]Howard LaFranchi, "Swaggart Scandal Casts Another Dark Shadow On TV Ministries," *Christian Science Monitor*, 26 February 1988, 6.

[13]Gustav Niebuhr, "Scandals' Ripples Rock TV Preachers," *Atlanta Journal*, 5 February 1989 (Newsbank SOC file 15: F1).

[14]Belanger (Newsbank: F1).

[15]Richard N. Ostling, "Worshipers on a Holy Roll." *Time*, 11 April 1988, 55.

occasion, he asserted, "If an individual's behavior is not Biblical and Christ-like, they ought to get out of the preaching business. They ought to fold it in and quit."[16] Still again, he noted, "It is impossible for me to stray sexually. My wife Frances is with me all the time. She goes to every crusade we go to. And if she doesn't go, I have several people who go with me. I'm never alone. I'm never by myself."[17]

Of course, all rhetors are constrained to some extent by prior statements they have made, but inasmuch as Swaggart's comments were made in close chronological proximity to his own scandal, inasmuch as these comments were usually given in combination with vehement attacks upon the other clerical culprits, and inasmuch as these comments ran directly counter to his subsequent actions, Swaggart would be hard pressed in his attempt to weave a defense that could incorporate these statements without appearing to promote hypocrisy and inconsistency.

THE VENDETTA

Swaggart's turn in the eye of the storm actually began with a less publicized conflict in 1986. In early July, Swaggart approached church officials with adultery accusations concerning another Pentecostal televangelist—Marvin Gorman. Gorman pastored a 5,000 member church in New Orleans, and he had a modest but rapidly growing television ministry in the southern region of the country. At the official inquest, Gorman admitted to an adulterous affair with one woman, but he vigorously denied involvement with any other women—a denial that prompted Swaggart to accuse him of lying. Gorman was defrocked of his preaching credentials, and subsequently lost his church and his television ministry. With those losses came the planting of seeds of

---

[16]Mike Dunne, Curt Eysink, and Doug Leblanc, "Swaggart Subject of Church Probe," *Baton Rouge Morning Advocate,* 20 February 1988 (Newsbank SOC file 15: D1).

[17]Ostling "Now It's Jimmy's," *Time,* 7 March 1988, 47.

revenge, seeds which would soon find occasion to blossom with whispers of a secret Swaggart hypocrisy.

Gorman's vendetta began with a legal assault. In February 1987, Gorman filed a $90 million defamation of character suit against Swaggart. The lawsuit accused Swaggart of "conspiring, plotting, and defaming"[18] against both Gorman and his ministry. Although the suit was initially thrown out, through appeals Gorman was able to revive it. Gorman and Swaggart would eventually settle out of court in 1994.

Gorman's second act of revenge against Swaggart was prompted by anonymous phone calls Gorman received concerning his rival. The source said that he had seen Swaggart and a prostitute enjoying each other's company on a number of occasions. After a few of these calls, Gorman hired private investigator Scott Bailey to follow Swaggart to verify the allegations. But it was Gorman's son Randy, substituting for Bailey, who successfully followed Swaggart to his rendezvous with Debra Murphree on October 17, 1987. Peering out of room twelve at the Travel Inn Motel, Randy took several photographs of Swaggart and Murphree entering the room. Once they were inside, Randy quickly let the air out of one of the tires on Swaggart's car and went to call his father. When Gorman arrived, Swaggart was fixing his flat.

According to Gorman, Swaggart and Gorman talked in his car for over two hours.[19] Swaggart admitted his indiscretions, and agreed to meet with Gorman, Gorman's lawyer, and Swaggart's wife and son the next day. At that meeting, Swaggart agreed to recant the statements he had made to the Assemblies of God leadership concerning Gorman's affairs, and he agreed to confess his own wrongdoing to ministry officials. But after four months had passed, and Swaggart had still not taken either action, Gorman took his accusations and the photographs to the executive presbytery of the Assemblies of God.

On February 18, Swaggart and his family were summoned to denomination headquarters in Springfield, Missouri. According to ministry officials, Swaggart confessed at this meeting that he had met

---

[18]Kaufman, 37.
[19]Dunne, Eysink, Leblanc (Newsbank: D1).

with a prostitute on a number of occasions, but that he had not engaged in sex. He also admitted that he had struggled against his fascination with pornography since childhood. That was all that anyone would ever hear concerning the details of the conversation between Swaggart and the presbytery.

Although not known until a week later, Debra Murphree claimed to be the prostitute in the pictures. She claimed that she had been meeting with Swaggart for about a year, and that he had never requested sex. Instead, he would pay between $25 and $50 to have her pose nude and fondle herself while he watched. Occasionally, he would masturbate as well.

In light of these incidents, three articles in *The Evangelist* magazine, written just before news of the scandal broke, took on a great ironic twist. In the February edition of the magazine, Swaggart described a dream God had recently given him. Richard N. Ostling of *Time* summarized the details: In the dream Jimmy and Frances attended a large meeting, where an Assemblies of God stage show was being promoted with magazines with obscene pictures in their centerfolds. Jimmy cried out in protest but is ignored. He bowed to weep, and when he looked up again, the auditorium was empty. The floor was littered with debris, which Jimmy started to collect. When someone asked him what he was doing, the evangelist responded, "I am trying to clean up the church. I am trying to clean up the church."[20]

The two other articles probably reached the one million subscribers to the magazine at approximately the same time as did the news of the scandal. In the March issue, the "Guest Forum" column was written by Christian media expert Ted Baehr on the subject "Was God a Nepotist? Protecting the Electronic Church From Wickedness."[21] On the adjoining page was an ad for the upcoming "Preachers' Rejuvenation Conference." In it, the writer began by lamenting that "the preacher today, even in Pentecostal and Charismatic circles, is in trouble. Scores

---

[20]Ostling, "Now It's Jimmy's," 48.

[21]Ted Baehr, "Was God a Nepotist? Protecting the Electronic Church from Wickedness," *The Evangelist* , March 1988, 35, 36.

are falling through immorality or just plain 'burnout.' "[22] Once again, Swaggart would be constrained by his previous comments, although this time, these statements would actually prove to be a rhetorical window of opportunity, as will be explained in the next chapter.

THE CAMPAIGN

On February 21, Swaggart delivered what was probably the most watched television sermon in history. As usual, the auditorium was filled to capacity, but this time the throngs included a large contingency of national media personnel. The service began with two songs by the choir, after which "Brother" Forrest Hall, District Secretary Treasurer of the Louisiana District Council of Assemblies of God, addressed the crowd to discuss the position of the state council on the situation. Most of his comments centered on reminding the audience of Swaggart's accomplishments for the Lord. "Let's not forget," he admonished, "all of the good things Swaggart has done in his life." He further informed the audience that the council was convinced of his sincerity and penitent heart. He concluded with the words, "Brother Swaggart, I believe I'm bringing you to a people who love you with all of their heart."[23] As Hall and Swaggart embraced, most of the people in the auditorium rose in a standing ovation for their fallen leader. The rhetorical campaign of Jimmy Swaggart was about to begin.

After a few moments of silence, Swaggart opened his Bible and began with these words: "Everything that I will attempt to say to you this morning will be from my heart." (See Appendix A for the text of the sermon.)

Swaggart's speech can be divided into six sections. Swaggart opened with an introduction designed to confirm the sincerity of his subsequent statements. In many different ways, he attempted to argue that, on this occasion, the people could be assured that he would tell the

---

[22]"Preachers Rejuvenation, 7-10 April 1988," *The Evangelist*, March 1988, 34.

[23]Forrest Hall in "The Jimmy Swaggart Broadcast," Trinity Broadcasting Network, 28 February 1988.

truth. Typical of the ideas in this section were these words: "I have always—every single time that I have stood before a congregation and a television camera—I have met and faced the issues head on. I have never sidestepped or skirted unpleasantries. I can do no less this morning."

It was apparent early on that there would be none of the usual dramatics in the Swaggart speaking style. There would be tears, and there would be moments of broken vocalization, but the shouting, the bodily gyrations, and the continual verbal movement towards climax after climax would be noticeably absent.

The second section dealt with the subject of Swaggart's relationship with the media. He claimed that the media had been fair in their treatment of him during this ordeal, and as a result, he had the highest respect for them. He even offered an expression of love for his "old nemesis—John Camp," the PBS reporter responsible for the 1983 documentary, "Give Me That Big Time Religion."

Section three was the longest of the sermon. Swaggart systematically apologized to all of the individuals and groups he had "wronged": his wife, his son and daughter-in-law, the Assemblies of God denomination, the Family Worship Center, the Jimmy Swaggart Bible College students and personnel, the television ministry staff, other television preachers, the "hundreds of millions that I have stood before in over a hundred countries of the world" (in revival meetings), and finally, his "Lord and Savior Jesus Christ." To each he concluded, "I have sinned against you, and I beg your forgiveness."

Section four detailed Swaggart's attempt to ascertain the cause of his indiscretions. He concluded that it must be a combination of two things: "Maybe Jimmy Swaggart has tried to live his entire life as though he were not human;" and "I did not seek the help of my brothers and my sisters in the Lord." He surmised that if he could have erased these two weaknesses from his life, then surely the "victory would have been mine." (See Appendix A.)

Section five was Swaggart's forecast of the future. He assured everyone that the ministry would continue and would thrive, but that he would "step out of the pulpit at this time for an indeterminate period of time."

Swaggart concluded by reading a lengthy confessional psalm traditionally thought to have been written by King David after his affair with Bathsheba. Near the end of his sermon, he commented: "I close this today with the words of another man that lived 3,000 years ago—and I started to say who committed sin that was worse than mine, but I take that back." (See Appendix A.)

Two incidents occurred during the service that were altered in some way for the television broadcast. First, a few people apparently rose to their feet and demanded to know exactly what immoral act Swaggart had committed. They were promptly escorted out of the building.

Secondly, it did seem that in the sound mixing, the sound of sobbing parishioners was enhanced beyond the reality of the situation. Certainly, there were many people in tears, but the sound was not as noticeable as the television version made it appear.

At the conclusion of the sermon, over one hundred members of the congregation came to the pulpit to embrace and pray over Swaggart. Their circle of compassion made for a compelling visual effect as the television cameras continued to roll.

What was the immediate response to the sermon? It seemed that for many critics and supporters alike, Swaggart's appearance of sincerity had been convincing. The Louisiana church officials, most of whom were present at the service, would reaffirm one day later that they were convinced of his repentant heart. Some members of the press praised him for not taking the elusive route taken by Bakker and others.[24] In addition, many of his supporters seemed convinced that their leader had done the right thing. Typical of comments made after the sermon, one Swaggart supporter said: "We listen to what is preached, not who's preaching it. We are practicing what Brother Swaggart says instead of

---

[24]Schultze, *Televangelism*, 104.

what he does;"[25] Another supporter noted, "I see him as any other human. Even in this fall, he set forth an example of repentance."[26]

The judgment of the Louisiana council of the Assemblies of God denomination was delivered the following day. The council expressed its belief that Swaggart had acted in a sincere, honest, and repentant manner. Therefore, they prescribed the following five point judgment:

(1) Swaggart must submit to a two-year program of rehabilitation.

(2) Swaggart could not preach for three months, except to fulfill his crusade obligations in foreign countries.

(3) Swaggart was to be relieved of all duties as co-pastor of the Family Worship Center for the three-month period.

(4) Swaggart would be supervised by the council, and would submit to weekly conferences with members of the council.

(5) Swaggart must submit to periodic reports on the progress he is making in regards to these matters.[27]

The council did not mention any particulars of the scandal and urged Swaggart and his staff to act laconically towards those who inquired into the details of the incident.

Swaggart would not preach again for three months, but his campaign to salvage his empire would still be in full swing during that time. The scandal had an immediate impact on the Swaggart ministries. In the first week after the apology, the ministries laid off over a hundred employees and halted all new construction. After the immediate casualties, damage seemed to stabilize, but it was too soon to tell how the incident would affect the ministries' life source—financial giving.

---

[25]Swaggart supporter Norma Svalmark, as quoted in Amy Wilson, "Jimmy Swaggart: The Forgiven," *Ft. Lauderdale Sun-Sentinel*, 12 March 1989, E-1.

[26]Denise Kalette, "Swaggart's 'Repentance' Key to Revival," *USA Today*, 23 February 1988, 1A.

[27]"Crisis in Baton Rouge."

Swaggart's attempt at salvaging his religious empire received its greatest challenge on March 27, when the national Assemblies of God leaders overruled the decision of the Louisiana presbytery, and instead imposed a one-year ban on Swaggart's preaching ministry. Despite the unexpected reversal, the reaction of Swaggart ministry officials was swift. Due to the inherent nature of television programming, many argued that swift action was absolutely required. As one Swaggart associate pointed out, "everyone around here knows that without Swaggart, there is no ministry. If he stays out a year, there will be no way to repair the damage."[28] Yet another official elaborated on the nuts and bolts dilemma the television ministry would face without the presence of their star: "If we cancel, we lose slots that have taken fifteen years to secure."[29] Thus, on March 29, Swaggart announced that he was resigning from the Assemblies of God denomination, and he would resume preaching on May 22, three months to the day after his confession sermon.

For those closest to Swaggart, this decision to leave the denomination seemed to carry greater consequence than the moral impropriety itself. Immediately after his pronouncement, almost a thousand church members left, as well as a number of key ministry officials. In addition, the Christian Broadcasting Network and the PTL (Praise the Lord) Network announced they would cancel the Swaggart programs, citing his unwillingness to obey denomination authorities as the primary reason. In addition, hundreds of students at the Jimmy Swaggart Bible College (JSBC) decided to attend denominational schools elsewhere rather than stay at Swaggart's school. The fact that the college itself reordained Swaggart after he gave up his credentials with the denomination did not seem to influence their decision.

In all, Swaggart lost approximately forty percent of his television viewers, almost half of his college students, three hundred positions in his ministry staff, and a third of his church attendees. By the midway

---

[28]Cathy Milam, "Aides Say Oral Cast Out Demons From Swaggart," *Tulsa World,* 1 April 1988 (Newsbank SOC file 42: E14).

[29]Belanger (Newsbank: F1).

point of his three month layoff, however, there was evidence that the trend was reversing. By the time he strode to the podium on May 21, many of his most ardent followers had already found the justification they needed to continue their support of Jimmy Swaggart.

Swaggart's rhetorical campaign during his now self-imposed sabbatical from preaching included at least twelve separate acts. The first occurred exactly one week after his apology sermon. According to "DM News," an organization that monitors the direct mail industry, one million form letters claiming to have been written by Swaggart himself were sent to supporters. The letter, which began, "It is a strange thing to say that I am writing this letter in victory, but that is exactly how I feel," devoted most of its space to a theological description of Swaggart's battle with Satan. Additional themes in the letter included Swaggart's courage in "baring all to my brethren," Swaggart's pain through this ordeal, in which he had "wept enough tears to swim in," and the improvement that would come about as a result of these incidents, by which Swaggart will be "a vessel used even more by the Holy Spirit."[30]

The second component of the campaign began two weeks later, as Swaggart's wife Frances and his son Donnie hosted a week long telethon. Frances outlined the crisis faced by the ministry, as she claimed that "in the last few weeks Satan has pressed his hand down strong to destroy these ministries." Thus, the majority of the time was spent requesting funds to help the ministry through these tough times. A tearful Donnie, who at one point looked toward the camera, and promised his father, "I will never leave you nor forsake you," requested that people send in at least fifty-three dollars in honor of his father's fifty-third birthday.[31]

A second letter was sent dated March 19. In this letter, Swaggart emphasized that every dollar sent to the Swaggart ministries went to feed and educate children around the world, and to spreading the

---

[30]Jimmy Swaggart, "A Personal Message," 28 February 1988, letter to supporters of the Jimmy Swaggart Ministries, 1, 2.

[31]"Swaggart's Wife, Son Ask Viewers for Cash," *Grand Rapids Press* , 16 March 1988, A6.

gospel through television. He also described a vision he received in which God commanded him to place his programming on every available station in the world. Finally, he concluded by contemplating his own blame in all of this. According to Swaggart, God reportedly said, "No, you have not failed. There were some things in your life I had to get out and other things I have to change. Then you will be able to do what I have told you to do."[32]

The next rhetorical act occurred in two parts of the April edition of *The Evangelist* magazine. In a letter entitlqed "I Just Want to Say, 'We love you,'" Jimmy and Frances began with: "During the last few weeks we have experienced more love than we ever thought possible." The letter used many of the same images and word pictures used in the apology sermon, but the main emphasis in this document was on Jimmy's work for the ministry, which led him to "total exhaustion week after week and month after month." Swaggart concluded by thanking his supporters for all of the love he had received, and assured them that "we will go through—and we will take millions of souls with us into the Kingdom of God."[33]

A more subtle defense of his character was presented in the April edition of the "Daily Devotional." In this apparent exegesis of a biblical passage, Swaggart chose the story of David and his battle with his enemies. The point Swaggart makes is that David is a "good example" for us when others try to perform evil upon us. He concluded, "Even if it seems no one else cares, we know God cares, and we can, like David, encourage ourselves in the Lord our God."[34]

---

[32]Swaggart, quoted in Jacqueline Case and Craig W. Cutbirth, "The Crucification of Jimmy Swaggart: A Religious Apologia," Division of Rhetoric and Public Address, Speech Communication Association Convention, 1 November 1990, 22.

[33]Jimmy Swaggart and Frances Swaggart, "I Just Want to Say, 'We Love You,'" "*The Evangelist*, April 1988, 12.

[34]Jimmy Swaggart, "The Word for Every Day," *The Evangelist*, April 1988, 10.

Swaggart's next rhetorical act took on a physical dimension. Through limited access media,[35] Swaggart publicized an exorcism by Oral Roberts on Swaggart's "demons of lust." According to fellow Assembly of God pastor Mike Evans, Oral Roberts told Swaggart that he saw "demons with long fingernails digging the flesh into his body."[36] The exorcism was apparently successful, and Swaggart told an associate that Roberts had "freed him from temptation."[37]

Although Swaggart held true to his promise not to preach for three months, he did appear on stage at least once during his layoff. During the April 10 service at the Family Worship Center, Swaggart led the choir in a rousing rendition of "He Set Me Free." The only thing he reportedly said during the service was "Give the Lord a hand of praise," but he did dance and jump around during his choir leading duties.

Another letter was sent out in mid-April. The message of this letter was that "it is fairly obvious that the devil tried to destroy this ministry," which is an act Satan inevitably perpetrates against any ministry attempting to do "world evangelism." Swaggart concluded by appealing for support "for the sake of the millions of souls who will die lost and spend eternity in hell."[38]

Just one week later, his partners and supporters received another letter and appeal for support. In this message, Swaggart emphasized the notions of spiritual battle and transformation. He claimed that those who are taking a "wait and see" attitude concerning financial support are actually doing exactly what Satan wants them to do. After claiming that unless he received additional financial support, the program will go off the air, Swaggart stated, "that will be exactly what Satan wants; is that what you want?"[39]

---

[35]Schultze, *Televangelism*, 232. Schultze describes how Swaggart uses limited access media, i.e. non syndicated sources. This extraordinary story did not reach the national press until well after its occurrence.

[36]Milam (Newsbank: E13).

[37]Milam (Newsbank: E13).

[38]Case and Cutbirth, 18, 25.

[39]Case and Cutbirth, 18, 26.

The second theme in this letter dealt with his personal transformation. He wrote that on May 22, "you will see a different Jimmy Swaggart. You will see a man with more compassion, more love, and more understanding." Swaggart claimed that this change will result because he "crawled to the foot of the cross to be broken and humbled."[40]

The May issue of *The Evangelist* continued Swaggart's attempt at receiving full forgiveness and restoration. In a column entitled "From Me to You," Swaggart repeated many of the themes he developed in earlier messages: spiritual battle, transformation, past ministry victories, comparisons with King David, and doctrinal screens, which this time had Swaggart proclaiming that he had been "crucified in the flesh."[41] By this point, it is unlikely that any of Swaggart's regular audience had missed his most common themes.

On May 2, Swaggart came close to breaking his vow not to preach for three months by taking center stage in an hour long nationally televised special. Set in a casual setting with no audience, Swaggart proclaimed that he had to raise six million dollars immediately to save his staggering ministries. The only theme that directly responded to his actions was again cast in a transformation narrative—his commitment to be less critical once he returned to the pulpit.

As May 22 neared, much of the correspondence included numerous references to Swaggart's climactic return for which all the Christian world waited. The hype was heightened by the guest speakers who were filling in at the Family Worship Center. On one occasion, the Reverend Al Trotter, who was filling in during Swaggart's absence, had this to say about the upcoming event: "Just one thing is agitating me and just one thing is filling me with nervous anticipation. That's for Sunday, May 22, to roll around and for the bishop to take the pulpit again."[42] After three months of communication acts designed to

---

[40]Case and Cutbirth, 26.
[41]Case and Cutbirth, 15, 16, 19.
[42]"Swaggart Didn't Preach," A6.

convince his followers to stay with the ship, it was time for Swaggart to put the finishing touches on his comeback campaign.

On the day of his return, Swaggart certainly did not disappoint the five thousand people present for his return. Emerging from behind a huge gray stage curtain to the accompaniment of a drum roll, Swaggart proceeded to recreate the form that had originally catapulted him to the top of the religious television charts. After leading the choir in two songs[43] (an act which was edited out of the televised version), Swaggart sat at the piano to play and sing two songs of his own: "We'll Talk It Over In the Bye and Bye," and "The Old Account Was Settled Long Ago." The audience gave him a strong ovation after each rendition.

Before Swaggart rose to preach, Frances Swaggart stood at the podium to make a few remarks. Typical of her comments was the statement, "I think (my love for humanity) has increased more than ever before because now when I look at people and their hurting, I can not only sense their hurt, I can feel their hurt. I can actually feel their pain." (See Appendix B) Just like her husband, Frances claimed to be transformed by this experience.

Finally, Swaggart ended his three month hiatus from preaching. Unlike his apology sermon, and unlike most of his layoff comments and correspondence, this sermon involved a return to the narrative verbal style. In this style, development of a coherent theme was subordinate to the turning of an especially witty phrase, delivered in an especially animated style. After such moments of verbal passion, Swaggart would drop down to a calm speaking style, as an eager audience awaited the next euphoric moment of preaching brilliance.

The theme was summarized in his choice of sermon text: "Brethren, I count not myself to have apprehended, but this one thing I do: forgetting those things which are behind and reaching forth unto those things which are before I press toward the mark for the prize of the high calling of God in Christ Jesus." (Phil. 3:13,14 New American

---

[43]Mike Dunne, "Evangelist Says He Will Put Past Behind Him," *Baton Rouge Morning Advocate*, 23 May 1988 (Newsbank SOC file 53: E12).

Standard Bible) He summarized as such in this statement: "Completely forgetting that which is past."

In the televised version of the sermon, Swaggart made two pleas for financial contributions. In both clips, Swaggart performed voiceovers accompanied with dramatic pictures from past revivals and crusades. He also argued that if there were to be future acts of global evangelization, then the people had to contribute.

The longest section of his sermon dealt with two dreams Swaggart professed to have had in the same night. The dreams, full of leviathan monsters and shadowy figures, will be narrated in detail in chapter five.

At the conclusion of the service, several hundred people rushed the podium to receive prayer for healing and to speak in tongues. Amid the excitement, two dramatic and rather unusual events occurred. At one point, a man approached Swaggart and embraced him in what seemed to be an act of admiration. As he let go, however, he simultaneously placed a document in Swaggart's hands; a document that turned out to be a court summons. The man was Reed Bailey, the private detective hired by Marvin Gorman. The document concerned the defamation suit filed by Gorman against Swaggart. According to Peter H. King of the *Los Angeles Times*, Swaggart was visibly upset at both the substance of the document and the timing of its delivery.[44]

The second incident occurred just moments later. As Frances spotted in the crowd a *Washington Post* reporter who had written an unflattering article about the Swaggarts, she began to shout criticisms at the reporter for his work. As the exchange began to capture the attention of those still in the building, Donnie attempted to move his mother away from the confrontation. As he did so, his mother shoved back and shouted, "Don't shove me!"[45] According to King, mother and son showed an unusual moment of anger towards one another.

As mentioned earlier, our focus has been on Swaggart's immediate audience, but to complete the composite of the rhetorical situation, we

---

[44]Peter H. King, "A Defiant Swaggart Returns to the Pulpit," *Los Angeles Times*, 23 May 1988, (Newsbank SOC file 53: E10).

[45]King (Newsbank: E11).

now turn to a consideration of the various auditor groups Swaggart had to address in his campaign.

AUDIENCES

In his text dealing with rhetorical criticism, James Andrews suggests that there are three things the critic must know about an audience: the listeners' knowledge, their group identification, and their receptivity to the speech and the topic.[46] We will consider these issues as we examine the five distinct audiences Swaggart had to consider during his campaign. Each presented unique challenges and opportunities.

Family Worship Center Attendees

Clearly, the listeners with the strongest bond to Swaggart were those who attended the church on a regular basis, which included college and ministry staff, Jimmy Swaggart Bible College students, and local citizens. They were the audience most likely to share his world view, who stood to be most influenced by his credibility, who most felt that they personally knew the rhetor, and who had the most to lose if this scandal brought Swaggart's complete downfall. Swaggart's departure would not only bring them intense confusion and dissonance as they tried to coordinate belief and reality, but they would also lose the source behind their weekly moments of ecstasy, when they would leave the world and its cares behind and come to hear Jimmy engage in rhetorical melodrama. Add to this the fact that the Swaggart ministries were the second largest employer in Baton Rouge, and it is likely that many, if not most, in the audience were extremely receptive to Swaggart's appeals. What they needed was a rationale, a way to coordinate their doctrine and their continued support for Swaggart. In any event, they certainly had strong motivation for seeking out such a rationale.

---

[46]James R. Andrews, *The Practice of Rhetorical Criticism* (New York: Longan, 1990), 29.

In terms of their knowledge and group identification, their commitment to Pentecostal doctrine in general and to the Assemblies of God in particular would play the central role in their response to the campaign. The next chapter will be entirely devoted to exploring what they believed, the extent to which they believed it, and how that belief was transformed into Swaggart's campaign to salvage his empire.

Assemblies of God Leadership

The group with the most immediate power over Swaggart's future was also the group facing the most acute dilemma. Not only was Swaggart the denomination's most shining star, but he was also its biggest contributor. In the year before the scandal, Swaggart placed over twelve million dollars in the denomination coffers devoted to missionary outreach. To an organization that values world evangelism as its *raison d'etre*, the importance of such charity could not be easily dismissed.

But this was also an organization that was nursing a black eye from the fall of its other favorite son—Jim Bakker. It was not lost on the media that the two most spectacular scandals occurred to men from the same denomination.

Finally, this group was constrained by its own actions in the past, and by its own church laws. Not only had they never given a penalty of less than one year for a moral lapse, but their own bylaws state that "indiscretions involving morals" required a rehabilitation period of at least two years.[47]

In the end, the composite of the rhetorical situation may not have allowed this audience to truly be receptive to Swaggart's message, for to grant Swaggart a lenient sentence would cast additional aspersions upon the greater good—the denomination. Of course, it is also likely that they sincerely believed that Swaggart's behavior precipitated a serious response from them.

---

[47]"More Trouble," 48.

The Media

As mentioned earlier, Swaggart was known for his fiery assaults on various religious, cultural and social groups. Over the years, one of his favorite targets was the "secular" media. Swaggart invariably blamed them for many of the evils he perceived in American life. He included teen suicide as one of those evils, as he explained in his sermon entitled "The New Evangelists:"

> I want you to understand where these people are coming from. Ninety-three percent—you see, the Devil doesn't like his rot to be uncovered, he doesn't like the lid pulled off his garbage—Ninety-three percent of media representatives do not attend church. Ninety-three percent have no church affiliation. Eighty-five percernt of media representatives, these new evangelists, admit that they are liberals, a term synonymous with secular humanist, which is a term synonymous with atheist or agnostic. . . . Are these new evangelists successful at propa-gating their religion? I'll tell you how successful they are. Everyday in the United States, 365 days a year, a thousand children, teenagers, attempt suicide. . . . The new evangelists, their new religion, secular humanism, to abolish God from our schools, our government, our homes, to abolish Christianity. What is the future? The die has been cast.[48]

Virtually every media description of Swaggart included a depiction of his confrontational approach to institutions and groups outside his own ideological association, so it was likely that many, if not most, of the journalists who covered the scandal were aware of Swaggart's public proclamations concerning their profession. This knowledge had to influence the level of objectivity that some of them brought to the situation.

---

[48]Harvey, 93.

Receptivity among media personnel was also unlikely due to the motive behind the relationship they shared with Swaggart. The press needed a story that the public would buy, and that story may or may not be favorable toward Swaggart. Even if one accepts the premise that the media are governed by a commitment to accuracy, this situation presented enough ambiguity to allow the press to engage in significant conjecture.

Swaggart's Regular Television Viewers

To consider the questions of group identification, receptivity and knowledge of Swaggart's television viewers, we must first consider exactly who was watching, and how the medium shared by rhetor and auditors affected the message. Thus, two questions will be addressed: (1) demographically, who watched the Jimmy Swaggart broadcast? (2) how did the delivery system—television, impact the way in which they process the messages they hear and see?

Swaggart's audience demographics are similar to most religious television audiences in that at least half of the audience was over fifty, the audience tended to be less educated than non-viewers, the South made up the largest geographic region of support, and the vast majority attended church on a regular basis.[49] What is different about Swaggart's audience is that it is equally divided by gender.[50] Additionally, many in Swaggart's audience are either Pentecostals themselves or at least sympathetic to a Pentecostal worldview.[51]

In terms of the impact of the medium on the situation, television possesses inherent characteristics that inevitably affect the viewer, as well as an inventory of tools of persuasion not available to the non-televised rhetor. There are at least three ways in which television inherently shape viewers and their responses. Initially, television

---

[49]Stewart M. Hoover, *Mass Media Religion* (Newbury Park: Sage Publications, 1988), 63-69.

[50]Hadden and Swann, 62.

[51]Harvey, 94.

inherently affects an audiences' ability to think carefully about the messages they are receiving. Most theorists concede that television is a communication medium that inhibits reflective thought. Schultze explains:

> As a technology . . . television does not accurately or easily communicate abstract or complex ideas. Unlike the printed word, which the reader can ingest intellectually at his own pace, the images on the tube keep running regardless of the ability to make sense of them. The viewer cannot stop to reflect upon what he has seen and heard except after the program is over.[52]

The reasons for this absence of reflection by television viewers are many, but two primary reasons are the visual nature of the medium, and the controlling programming metaphor of entertainment. Television's reliance upon visual images, as Kathleen Hall Jamieson correctly argues in *Eloquence in an Electronic Age*, gives it an associative influence, and thereby makes it difficult for the viewer to demand evidence or to judge arguments in traditional ways.[53] Perhaps it is because the viewer generally operates under the belief that the camera cannot lie, and thus visual images are not subjected to the careful scrutiny that may be given to other forms of argument.

Media critic Neil Postman suggests that additional support for television's inability to promote careful thinking can also be shaped out of an examination of the profit motive behind television programming. As a result, the paradigm of programming can be summed up in one word: entertainment. This point is made clear in this summary from Postman's heralded book, *Amusing Ourselves to Death*:

---

[52]Quentin Schultze, "TV and Evangelism: Unequally Yoked?," *The Agony of Deceit* edited by Michael Horton (Chicago: Moody Press, 1990), 191.

[53]Kathleen Hall Jamieson, *Eloquence in an Electronic Age* (New York: Oxford University Press, 1988).

... television's way of knowing is uncompromisingly hostile to typography's way of knowing; that television's conversations promote incoherence and triviality; that the phrase "serious television" is a contradiction in terms; and that television speaks in only one persistent voice—the voice of entertainment.[54]

The second characteristic of television that necessarily affected Swaggart's campaign is the medium's tendency to create an artificial relationship between televised rhetor and viewer. Consider that television viewing is often a private experience, with no one involved except the viewer in the seat and the face on the screen. Added to this is the ability that the camera possesses to bring us in close proximity to the rhetor. As a result, the televised rhetor can serve as the faithful companion. He is there every week at the same time; she expresses love for us no matter what we do or say; he always gives us ways to improve our present condition.

Finally, television creates the appearance of reality, masking the extent to which it is actually a crafting of images. The camera may not lie, but what it does not show is as important as what it shows. What is edited out, what is added in, what is enhanced, all contribute to the final effect, and it does so because our visual senses tell us that what we are seeing is what actually is happening. As mentioned earlier, there is evidence that suggested that Swaggart significantly altered the apology service for an even more compelling televisual experience. Unfortunately, when a viewer is watching what seems to be a linear experience, the very fact of the viewing becomes an argument in and of itself.

Situational Television Viewers

Certainly, many viewers tuned in just because of the scandal situation. For most of them, the potential entertainment value of the rhetoric was the motivating factor. As Schultze pointed out, they were not disappointed: "(the apology sermon) was fabulous television, more

---

[54]Neil Postman, *Amusing Ourselves to Death* (New York: Penguin, 1985), 80.

compelling than most soap made-for-TV films and more dramatic than any evening soap opera."[55]

It is unlikely that this group would be receptive to the overall goals that Swaggart had in mind. Even if they were, persuasive success was unlikely because of the absence of a shared worldview and body of information that Swaggart could draw upon, and because this audience would not have access to the remainder of the rhetorical campaign. For those people who did not suffer from those deficiencies, however, doctrinal arguments would play a key role.

---

[55]Schultze, *Televangelism*, 39.

4

THE RESPONSE:
THEOLOGY AS ARGUMENT

Just because Jimmy Swaggart believes in God doesn't mean that God
does not exist

—Walker Percy[1]

WALKER PERCY NOTWITHSTANDING, THERE WERE MANY PEOPLE
listening to Swaggart's rhetorical campaign who were vitally interested
in what Swaggart believed. As the shared belief and subsequent
understanding passed between speaker and audience, there was little
doubt about Swaggart's overt stance: "I have no one to blame but
myself. I do not lay the fault or the blame of the charge at anyone else's
feet. For no one is to blame but Jimmy Swaggart. I take the responsibility. I take the blame. I take the fault" (see Appendix A). This, however,
was by no means the conclusion at which his audience would arrive.
Indeed, by the end of his campaign, most of this doctrinal community
would be convinced that the devil, demons, pornographers, and even
the audience members themselves were to blame for Swaggart's failure.
In fact, virtually everyone but Swaggart would ultimately feel the sting
of doctrine turned defense witness.

This chapter will explore the perceived rationality of Swaggart's
arguments as seen through the eyes of his primary audience. Using
Stephen Toulmin's model for diagramming and analyzing informal
argument, we will examine Swaggart's theological case for his restoration. As we will see, his case was developed with the help of his

---

[1]Walker Percy, "Science, Language, Literature," *Signposts in a Strange Land*, ed.
Patrick Samway (New York: Farrar, 1992), 159.

doctrinal community. For that reason, it was largely missed by outside observers altogether.

THE TOULMIN PARADIGM

Stephen Toulmin's paradigm offers the critic a strategy by which to search for the unspoken elements of public argument. Specifically, his notion of the warrant allows the critic to explore the assumptions that must be shared between speaker and audience if an argument is to be accepted. In that these warrants are often unspoken, the Toulmin system, as Hart explains, "encourages us to search for such 'missing' elements, since examining the unstated in discourse provides the most subtle understanding of speaker-audience relationships."[2]

There are three central parts to the Toulmin model. Toulmin defines "claims" simply as "assertions put forward publicly for general acceptance."[3] Claims answer the question "what are you trying to prove?" Toulmin discusses only the concept of "subclaims,"[4] but we will expand upon Hart's revision of claim types. Hart speaks of "major claims," which he defines as the "broadest, most encompassing, statements made by the speaker." Major claims function at a level of abstraction higher than all other statements the speaker makes. They represent what the speaker hopes will become the "residual" message in listeners' minds (that is, the main thoughts remembered when the details of a message have been forgotten). Finally, major claims are frequently repeated or restated in the message.[5]

Swaggart's major claim became synonymous with the overall goal of his rhetorical campaign. Swaggart's major claim was, "I am worthy of forgiveness and continued support." Success for Swaggart rested upon the hope that all lines of reasoning lead down this road.

---

[2] Hart, *Modern*, 143.
[3] Stephen Toulmin, Richard Rieke, and Allan Janik, *An Introduction to Reasoning* (New York: Macmillan, 1984), 29.
[4] Toulmin, 75.
[5] Hart, *Modern* 142.

Although not mentioned by Hart, every major claim needs minor claims. Minor claims will be defined as conclusions that, if accepted, support the veracity of the major claim. Toulmin refers to the second part of his paradigm as the "grounds." He defines grounds as the "specific facts relied on to support a given claim."[6] They answer the question, "What have you got to go on?" Grounds are almost always verbalized by the speaker and, as is the case with claims, are often repeated across various speaking contexts.

The final and most important part of the model is called warrants. Defined by Toulmin as "statements indicating how the facts on which we agree are connected to the claim or conclusion now being offered,"[7] warrants reveal why the grounds justify the claim. It is here that speaker and audience come together, often in unspoken shared meaning. It is here that Swaggart called upon his audience's belief in and their Pentecostal interpretation of the Bible to connect the facts and his goal of full restoration.

In order fully to understand the nature of any particular public argument situation, it is important that the critic consider how the speaker and audience come to accept anything as true. Thus, it is necessary to consider the epistemological premises that informed this audience's ideas and beliefs.

EPISTEMOLOGICAL PRESUPPOSITIONS

Members of Swaggart's primary audience were churchgoers, and more specifically, Pentecostal churchgoers. Even more specifically, a significant part of Swaggart's primary audience were members of the largest of the Pentecostal denominations, the Assemblies of God. This means that a correlation should be found between Swaggart's beliefs, and the beliefs of Pentecostalism in general and Assembly of God adherents in particular.

---

[6]Toulmin, 38.
[7]Toulmin, 45.

Swaggart and his audience shared at least four epistemological presuppositions. Each of these affect how they come to regard something as true or untrue, right or wrong. Each would have a major impact on the formation of Swaggart's defense of his character.

First, *the Bible is the inerrant word of God. Everything that the Bible says is true and nothing that contradicts the Bible is true.* This is the starting point to an understanding of this doctrinal community. The first tenet of the Assemblies of God statement of faith declares: "We believe the Bible is the inspired and only infallible and authoritative Word of God."[8] Thus, any argument that is warranted upon a basis of a biblical passage is bound to be accepted, as long as it is in line with an accurate interpretation of that passage. In terms of assessing the accuracy of any particular interpretation, Swaggart offers this advice: "There is such a thing as false doctrine and there is such a thing as sound doctrine. Sound doctrine is simply what is preached and practiced according to the Word of God by preachers and teachers who have rightly divided the Word of Truth."[9]

This indicates that there is a dimension of personal credibility to assessing sound biblical interpretation. The listener must determine if the preacher is one who is likely to divide the word of truth rightly. How does a listener know if the preacher is capable of this? By the results that his preaching and teaching bring. He noted:

> In other words, one preacher will teach one doctrine and another preacher will teach the exact opposite. But both men will claim to be Scriptural! This often leaves the layperson in a quandary. Both claim to be Scriptural, and yet one (or both) may be wrong. Consequently . . . you must determine if the doctrine is profitable. . . . In other words, you can judge doctrine by its results.[10]

---

[8]Assemblies of God, *Who We Are and What We Believe* (Springfield, MO: Gospel Publishing House, 1982), 17.

[9]Swaggart, *Straight Answers*, 5.

[10]Swaggart, *Straight Answers*, 6.

At first glance, the listener may be tempted to decide that Swaggart did not rightly "divide the Word of Truth," since it did not produce results in his own life. But as the analysis of the particular strains of argument will illustrate, this audience was much more likely to place emphasis upon the emotional power of the preaching, and upon the quantitative results of the evangelistic outreach when evaluating the results of a preacher. Thus the first presupposition in how this audience comes to know what they know is that the Bible is the ultimate and authoritative source of all knowledge.

Second, *a non-Christian, or an unbeliever, cannot fully discern truth as clearly as a Christian*. Based upon texts such as 1 Cor. 2:14, "But a natural man does not accept the things of God; for they are foolishness to him, and he cannot understand them, because they are spiritually appraised," Swaggart and his audience would possess a *prima facie* suspicion of any statement, accusation, or argument that originated from someone outside their religious tradition. Even when that unbeliever is an informed and learned individual, the Christian should doubt their veracity, for 1 Tim. 3:7 reminds the reader that the unbeliever is "always learning, and never able to come to the knowledge of the truth." Swaggart reminds his readers of this fact from this very verse on the first page of *Straight Answers To Tough Questions*.[11]

Incidentally, for Swaggart this epistemological premise becomes a minor claim in and of itself, often in very subtle ways. For example, when Swaggart mentioned in the apology sermon that Ted Koppel's "Nightline" report was "at least as fair and as honest, as he, the spokesman for this world-famed news program, could make it" (see Appendix A), Swaggart was offering much more than a conciliatory word of praise for Koppel. To Swaggart's primary audience, the operational phrase was "as fair and as honest as he could make it," for they all knew that as an unbeliever, Koppel's ability to find the honest truth was significantly impaired by his spiritual condition.

---

[11]Swaggart, *Straight Answers*, 3.

Third, *Spirit-filled Christians do receive direct revelations and prophecies from God*. When responding to the question "Does God speak to people today?" Swaggart emphatically responded in the affirmative. He then explained that God speaks today through at least seven oracles: by speaking through an audible voice, by appearing directly to men, by speaking through angels, by speaking through dreams and visions, by laying impressions upon a person's heart, by speaking through events, and by speaking through his word, which Swaggart labels the "greatest" method of God's communication with human beings.[12] Swaggart would suggest God had spoken to him through most of these conduits,[13] although he tends to be skeptical of the claims of direct revelation from other Christian leaders.[14]

Margaret Poloma's research into the world of the Assemblies of God denomination confirms that Swaggart was not alone in his belief in direct revelation. She documented that ninety-eight percent of Assembly of God pastors indicated that their church services included public acts of prophecy[15] at least once in the past six months,[16] while forty-five percent reported at least biweekly experiences of prophecy in their churches.[17]

How does one know if the revelation or prophecy is really from God? Swaggart reduces the guidelines for determining the authenticity

---

[12]Swaggart, *Straight Answers*, 168, 169.

[13]Swaggart suggests this generally in *Straight Answers*, 171. In addition, there are testimonials of his receiving revelation in different ways. His childhood revelation of the prophecy of Hiroshima came through God actually taking over Swaggart's body and voice (Swaggart, *To Cross*, 44), while an audible, specific and clear voice told him of his call to preach the Gospel through television (Swaggart, "God's Priorities," *The Evangelist*, April 1988, 10). In addition, his comeback sermon included a revelation from God in a dream. See Swaggart in "The Jimmy Swaggart Broadcast," 22 May 1988 (see Appendix B: 229-232).

[14]Swaggart, *Straight Answers*, 163-167.

[15]Poloma defines "prophecy" as "a gift of the Holy Spirit through which a person speaks in the name of God by giving an exhortation, reporting a vision, providing a revelation, or interpreting a glossolalaic utterance." See Margaret M. Poloma, *The Assemblies of God at the Crossroads* (Knoxville: University of Tennessee Press, 1989), 27.

[16]Poloma, 83.

[17]Poloma, 194.

of revelation two principles: consistency with the teachings of Scripture, and impact upon the life and work of the ministry.[18] If it is biblical and if it is produces godly results, the observer can be sure that it was indeed a heavenly revelation.

Fourth, some Christians are chosen and called by God for specific purposes, and as such, are worthy of receiving an attentive hearing by their audience on the subject of their calling. One of the direct revelations many Pentecostal preachers report receiving from God is a divine call to either a specific kind of ministry or a specific place for ministry. Swaggart received his general call to preach during his childhood days, but his specific call came on July 1, 1985, when God told him that he was to preach the gospel to the entire world via television.[19] During his rhetorical campaign, Swaggart often spoke of this call: "My calling has not been taken away; if anything, it has intensified."[20] On another occasion, he said, "As Peter was called to the Jews and as the Apostle Paul was called to the Gentiles, I have been called to perform a specific work at a specific moment in time."[21] On still another, he asserted, "I can still hear the words of the Master: 'Feed my Sheep.' "[22] This final reference was be recognizable to Swaggart's audience as a parallel to Christ's words to Peter when he received his call to evangelism as recorded in John 21:17.

This doctrine of a divine calling serves both as an argument in and of itself, and as epistemological grounds for other arguments. As an argument in and of itself, Swaggart's audience would accept that a call from God is permanent, even after scandal. If a call to perform televised world evangelism is permanent, then it is to be heeded, even after momentary lapses in moral judgment.

As an epistemological presupposition, it serves to enhance the authority of the speaker. If God gave Swaggart this calling, then God must also provide him with the necessary knowledge as to how this task

---

[18]Swaggart, *Straight Answers*, 163-167.

[19]Swaggart, "God's Priorities," 10.

[20]Swaggart, quoted in Case and Cutbirth, 15.

[21]Swaggart, "God's Priorities," 10.

[22]Swaggart, "A Personal Message," 2.

is to be accomplished. Swaggart is God's expert on earth in the area of world evangelism. In a community that accepted a strong authoritarian relationship between leaders and those who are led, such an expert is not to be discarded lightly. When Swaggart talks about world evangelism, the audience should listen.

When placed together, these presuppositions make clear that Swaggart, who hears directly from God, including a call to world television evangelism, is in a strong epistemological position. When combined with his use of the Bible to justify his arguments, there is little reason for this doctrinal community to deny Swaggart his claims.

DOCTRINAL ARGUMENTS

Swaggart called upon ten doctrinal argument to make his case. Each of these arguments will be examined through the lens of the Toulmin model. At times Swaggart encapsulated his warrants in one particular biblical passage, while at other times the link between grounds and claims were implied from a number of verses or from Pentecostal theology in general. When possible, I have included anecdotal evidence of how the audience accepted Swaggart's usage of these arguments. To illustrate that acceptance, I have occasionally relied on Charles R. Fontaine and Lynda K. Fontaine's book, *Jimmy Swaggart: To Obey God Rather Than Men*.[23] Charles Fontaine is a Texas church janitor who had never met Swaggart. He and his wife wrote the book at the conclusion of Swaggart's rhetorical campaign as their defense of Swaggart's decision to return to preaching in three months and thereby give up his Assembly of God credentials. Only a small number of these books were printed because, according to the Fontaines, they wrote it under the direction of the Holy Spirit with the sole purpose of distributing them to Assembly of God officials and pastors. The end result is useful to this study in that the Fontaines give evidence of their understanding and acceptance of a number of the arguments discussed in this section.

---

[23]Charles R. Fontaine, and Lynda K. Fontaine, *Jimmy Swaggart: To Obey God Rather Than Men* (Crockett: Kerusso, 1989).

The Doctrine of Sin

Both the secular press and Assembly of God officials were among the many who praised Swaggart for his willingness to admit his wrongdoing. Unlike the Nixons, Harts, and Bakkers of this world, Swaggart demonstrated the moral fortitude to come forward and confess the error of his ways. What the admirers may not have realized, however, was that in the simple act of naming his deed a sin, Swaggart was invoking an entire systematized approach to wrongdoing that could only help him in his attempt at restoration.

Grounds ------->Warrants -------------> Minor Claims -----------> Major Claims			
I have sinned.	"For all have sinned and fall short of the glory of God." (Rom. 3:23)	The reality and seriousness of my deeds are replicated in you every day.	I am worthy of forgiveness and continued support.
	Implied: All sin is equal in God's eyes.		

Swaggart wasted no time in establishing the grounds for this argument. Less than two minutes into his apology sermon, he explained, "I do not call it a mistake, a mendacity; I call it a sin" (see Appendix A). In the next twenty minutes, he referred to his deeds fourteen times, each time calling it "sin," or as an action, that he "sinned." This consistency continued throughout his rhetorical campaign, as each subsequent reference to his scandalous activity was labeled only as his "sin."

Swaggart's primary audience believed at least two axioms about the doctrine of sin that served as warrants to his claims. First, Swaggart's audience was convinced that sin is a universal experience. Based on verses such as Rom. 3:23 mentioned above, they readily accepted the argument that the act of committing sin is certainly the one thing in which they, Swaggart and auditors alike, all share. As declared in the "The Priceless Corner" section of *The Evangelist*, "Man is a sinner and sin has separated him from God! 'For there is not a man upon earth that doeth good and sinneth not' (Eccles. 7:20)."[24] Placed into this context, each auditor had to acknowledge that although they may not have masturbated in a seedy hotel room while a prostitute fondled herself, every individual auditor, as a member of the human race, had sinned. Thus, the claim follows that the reality of Swaggart's deed is not unique, since all humanity commits deeds that fall within the "sin" category.

Swaggart drew upon a second doctrinal presupposition that would bridge the gap between grounds and claims. Not only did he consider sin a universal experience, but in terms of magnitude or seriousness, he argued that all particular sins were equally abhorrent in God's eyes. The proponents of this idea could not call upon a verse that clearly states it, but they imply it from such verses as James 2:10, "For whoever keeps the whole law but becomes guilty in one point, he has become guilty of all." Swaggart, his audience, and most Protestant Evangelicals for that matter, would argue that even one sin "separates us from God,"[25] so an act with a prostitute or delivering an ill-spoken expletive, for example, are equal in severity and consequence. Both had to be confessed and both had to be forgiven if the sinner hoped to enter the kingdom of heaven.

Securing that forgiveness was the logical next step in the progression, but the mere fact that the doctrine of sin suggested to the audience that Swaggart was no worse than they were was, in itself, a powerful case for forgiveness and restoration. As one supporter responded, "I see him as any other human."[26] Such a point of view certainly weakened the seriousness of Swaggart's transgression.

---

[24]"The Priceless Corner," *The Evangelist*, May/June 1991, 5.
[25]Assemblies of God, 17.
[26]Kalette, 1A.

Repentance, Forgiveness, Redemption

As mentioned earlier, many of these arguments included warrants that were understood by the audience but unstated by the rhetor. In contrast, Swaggart's usage of this argument included numerous examples of his stating both grounds and warrants. In the apology sermon, Swaggart directly addressed God: "I have sinned against you, my Lord. And I would ask that your precious blood would wash and cleanse every stain, until it is in the sea of God's forgetfulness, never

---

Grounds------------->Warrants------------->Minor Claims------------>Major Claims

Grounds	Warrants	Minor Claims	Major Claims
I have confessed my sin to Christ.	"But God shows his love for us, in that while we were sinners, Christ died for us. (Rom.5:8)	Christ has forgiven me of my sins. Christ has forgotten about my sin.	I am worthy of forgiveness and continued support.
	"If we confess our sins, he is faithful and just to forgive us our sins, and to cleanse us from all unrighteousness. (I John1:9)	You should treat me as Christ would.	
	"For I will be merciful to their iniquities, and I will remember their sins no more." (Heb. 8:12)		
	"You will know them by their fruits." (Matt.5: 16)		

to be remembered against me anymore" (see Appendix A). The sea metaphor is a reference to a classic hymn with which Swaggart's audience would be well acquainted.

At the conclusion of the apology sermon, Swaggart quoted from the confessional prayer of David after his affair with Bathsheba. As will be explained in the following chapter on narrative, Swaggart would make much use of the lives of David and Peter during his rhetorical campaign, since it was after their moments of scandalous behavior and subsequent repentance that these two biblical heroes performed their mightiest works for God.

There were four components of Swaggart and his audience's shared doctrinal understanding that served as warrants for this particular argument. First, the cornerstone of their understanding of spiritual reality was the work of Christ on the cross to deal with the problem of sin. As proclaimed in the denominational statement of faith, this audience and rhetor believe that "the only means of our being cleansed from sin is through repentance and through faith in the precious blood of Christ."[27] Of importance to understanding Swaggart was that this forgiveness is not only the medium by which one becomes related to Christ, but it is also the medium by which a Christian maintains a good standing in that relationship.[28]

If the confession of sin is authentic, then the next two warrants promise the solution to the problem of sin. According to this doctrine, the Christian is promised two things after confession: God will forgive their sin, and God will forget their sin. As the Fontaines asserted,

> When Jimmy Swaggart repented, the Bible says God forgave him, cleansed him from all his unrighteousness, then supernaturally forgot his sin. At that point, for that sin, it was over. God forgave and forgot. By definition, then, there cannot be

---

[27]Assemblies of God, 18.
[28]Swaggart, *Straight Answers*, 73.

additional punishment after forgiveness that God ordains because He has forgotten the sin.[29]

Clearly, Swaggart hoped that the same amnesia would afflict his audience, for a sin forgotten is certainly a sin forgiven.

One final piece of the puzzle is needed for this argument. It may be true that God forgives and forgets sin after an authentic confession and repentance of that sin, but how are observers able to discern the sincerity of such confessions? In a message in the May 1988 issue of *The Evangelist*, Swaggart reminded his readers of the twofold answer to that very question:

(1) Has the person truly repented? If he has, his repentance will bear fruit; in other words, there will be evidence of repentance.

(2) When he comes back to the pulpit, the following evidence will be obvious: the Holy Spirit will be present, the message will be of God and touched by a brokenness and a compassion from heaven. These are signs of repentance and restoration.[30]

Months later, the Fontaines applied this concept of fruit inspection to the post-scandal life of Jimmy Swaggart:

The perfect example of this is Jimmy Swaggart himself. While he was off the air for three months, to most of us his observable fruit was only his written word in his letters and magazine, *The Evangelist*. With his return to the pulpit, it is obvious the anointing is on his ministry even heavier than before. . . .[31]

---

[29]Fontaine, 30.
[30]Dunne, "Swaggart to Oversee" (Newsbank: E8).
[31]Fontaine, 34.

What this final warrant provided for Swaggart's audience was a paradigm by which "objectively" to determine his sincerity. If there are results, such as people making decisions for Christ, if there is obvious emotional power in the preaching, and if there are specific manifestations of the Holy Spirit, such as glossolalia, then one can be assured that the confession and repentance is genuine.

Was this argument effective? With comments by supporters such as, "even in this fall, he set forth an example of repentance,"[32] there does seem to be evidence of effectiveness. But perhaps Swaggart's son Donnie best explained why this argument was persuasive when he forcefully proclaimed, "if there is no forgiveness for Jimmy Swaggart, there's no forgiveness for you either."[33] Indeed, perhaps the most important reason to forgive Swaggart was that it reminded others of the possibility that they too may be forgiven.

Baptism of the Holy Spirit And Glossolalia

Towards the end of Swaggart's comeback sermon, something happened that was rather unusual for a televised Swaggart service. Although the edited version did not show Swaggart's face during the event, there was no doubting what occurred: Swaggart spoke in tongues.[34] This "form of nondiscursive prayer in an unintelligible language, which from a linguistic viewpoint, is meaningless but phonologically structured,"[35] or "glossolalia" as the Koine Greek

---

[32]Kalette, 1A.

[33]Robert Wuthnow, "Religion and Television: The Public and the Private," *American Evangelicals and the Mass Media*, ed. Quentin J. Schultze (Grand Rapids: Academie, 1990), 211.

[34]There are seven camera stations within the Family Worship Center. At the time Swaggart spoke in tongues, the editor choose the shot from behind the platform. Thus, someone unacquainted with the practice of glossolalia could have decided that Swaggart said something that was simply mumbled in the television broadcast. But the vocalizations that Swaggart makes when he speaks in tongues are very distinct; the vocalizations in the comeback sermon are the same that Swaggart repeatedly made while speaking in tongues at the 1991 San Diego crusade, which this researcher attended.

[35]Poloma, 27.

language refers to it, was highly unusual in a televised, edited Swaggart

Grounds------------->	Warrants ------------>	Minor Claims ---------->	Major Claims
I spoke in tongues	"And they were all filled with the Holy Spirit and began to speak with other tongues." (Acts 1:4) i.e. Only those that are filled with the Holy Spirit are able to speak in tongues. "And God, who knows the heart, bore witness to them, giving them the Holy Spirit." (Acts 15:14) i.e. Only those that are right with God are filled with the Holy Spirit.	I am right with God.	I am worthy of forgiveness and continued support.

sermon. But after the scandal broke, there is evidence that Swaggart's practice of glossolalia increased significantly. Once again, a simple act, when combined with a shared meaning between rhetor and audience, served as a powerful character witness.

When suggesting guidelines for finding a church, Swaggart stated that the church should "stress, preach, and teach the mighty baptism in the Holy Spirit with the evidence of speaking with other tongues as the spirit gives them utterance."[36] Poloma points out that speaking in tongues is the most important religious experience for Assemblies of God ministers, with ninety-seven percent stating they speak in tongues at least once a week.[37] Sixty-seven percent of Assembly of God church members stated that they have spoken in tongues at least once.[38]

Discussion of glossolalia cannot proceed without a discussion of the baptism in the Holy Spirit. This baptism is defined by R.A. Torrey as that act in which "the Spirit of God comes upon a believer, taking possession of his faculties, imparting to him gifts not naturally his own, but which qualify him for the service to which God has called him."[39] Although Torrey never specified exactly which gifts were imparted through this experience, Pentecostals have traditionally embraced the belief that glossolalia was the evidence of the baptism of the Holy Spirit. This point is made clear in two of the statements in the Assemblies of God statement of faith:

> We believe that the baptism in the Holy Spirit is granted to all believers who ask for it. We further believe this experience is distinct from and follows the new birth, that it was the normal experience of New Testament Christians, and that it brings an enduement of power for Christian living and service. (Lk. 24:49; Acts 1:4, 8; 2:4; 10:44-46; 15:8, 9).
>
> We believe the baptism of believers in the Holy Spirit is witnessed by the initial physical sign of speaking with other tongues as the Spirit of God gives them utterance. (Acts 2:4, I Cor. 12:4-10, 28).[40]

In short, the Christian is given the Holy Spirit during this second baptism, which empowers him or her to live a godly life. If those

---

[36]Swaggart, *Straight Answers*, 145.

[37]Poloma, 12.

[38]Ibid.

[39]Torrey is quoted in Robert G. Gromacki, *The Modern Tongues Movement* (Nutley: Presbyterian and Reformed, 1977), 98, 99.

[40]Assemblies of God, 18.

Christians turn away from God in any way, they lose the Holy Spirit, and thus would need another baptism in the Holy Spirit in order to live a successful and powerful Christian life.

Once again, the audience is given a tangible way to determine whether an individual is living a life that is right with God. If those persons are living a clean life, and if they are capable of speaking in tongues, then they must possess the Holy Spirit, which means their life is presently right with God.

Evangelism as Raison D'etre

At times, Swaggart's attempt to establish the grounds for this argument were somewhat subtle. For example, the opening words of his comeback sermon included a simple reminder of the magnitude of his evangelistic influence: "I have stood before some of the largest crowds in the world but I guess I stand now with more fear and trembling than I have ever before in my life" (see Appendix B). At other times, he stated the grounds more directly. After offering his pleas

Grounds ---------->	Warrants ------------>	Minor Claims ---------->	Major Claims
I am the most effective evangelist in the world today.	"Go therefore and make disciples of all the nations." (Matt. 28:18) Implied: Evangelism is the most vital task in the world.	To restore me is to affirm your commitment to world evangelism.	I am worthy of forgiveness and continued support.

for forgiveness to six other groups of people, Swaggart turned his apology sermon tears towards "the hundreds of millions that I have stood before in over a hundred countries of the world and I've looked into the cameras and so many of you with a heart of loneliness, needing help, have reached out to this minister of the gospel as a beacon of light (see Appendix A)."

Later in the apology sermon, Swaggart assured the audience that the ministry would go on, in order that "we will continue to take this gospel of Jesus Christ all over the world" (see Appendix A). In future segments of his rhetorical campaign, Swaggart stated "we will go through—and we will take millions of souls with us into the Kingdom of God,"[41] and pleaded for support "for the sake of the millions of souls who will die lost and spend eternity in hell."[42] One other *Evangelist* promotion asks the rhetorical question, "Why does the Jimmy Swaggart telecast have the largest audience in America and the world?"[43]

Swaggart's primary audience would consider the evangelization of the non-Christian to be their *sine qua non*. The Assembly of God statement of faith lists it first under its "church and its mission" section.[44] In fact, they conclude the entire document with a section entitled "What About You?" which challenges readers concerning their own spiritual condition.[45] In addition, Swaggart concluded in one of his earlier books that evangelism, or "soul-winning" as it is called, is the primary task of any local church.[46]

Why do Pentecostals, as well as many other Christians, consider world evangelism as their most important activity? It is based upon two other doctrinal premises: (1) the belief in a literal hell, and; (2) a strong rejection of the Calvinistic notions of irresistible grace and unconditional election. This doctrinal community is fond of proclaiming "If we don't tell them, they won't get told,"[47] and of imagining those who will

---

[41]Swaggart, "I Just Want To Say," 12.
[42]Swaggart, quoted in Case and Cutbirth, 25.
[43]"Why Does the Jimmy Swaggart Telecast Have the Largest Audience in America and the World?," *The Evangelist*, Jan. 1988: 60.
[44]Assemblies of God, 19.
[45]Assemblies of God, 23.
[46]Swaggart, *Straight Answers*, 148.
[47]Jimmy Swaggart, "Our Upcoming Telethon is Our Most Important One Ever," *The Evangelist*, January 1988, 32.

end up in hell if the Christians do not engage in their primary task.[48] This directly contradicts the Calvinistic view that God will draw those whom he chooses, regardless of the will of those individuals or the actions of other individuals. Thus, the ultimate claim that the audience should continue to support Swaggart naturally followed their belief that world evangelism is the most urgent task and a belief that Jimmy Swaggart is the Samson of laborers in that effort. The options are either to deny Swaggart forgiveness, and thus send millions to their doom in hell, or allow him to return to his task, which, according to Swaggart, was given him by God: "God called me for world evangelism."[49]

The Blessed Hope

The groundwork for this eschatological argument was laid long before Swaggart's scandal problems. In 1986, Swaggart unveiled a plan to take his program to every nation on earth. The plan, entitled "D-Day

Grounds ------------>	Warrants ------------->	Minor Claims ---------->	Major Claims
My television program is the only hope for taking the Gospel to all the nations.	"And this gospel of the kingdom shall be preached in the whole world for a witness to all the nations, and then the end shall come." (Matt. 24:14)	If I am not restored, the second coming of Christ will be delayed.	I am worthy of forgiveness and continued support.

or Delay," promised to be the instrument which would usher in the blessed hope: the literal second coming of Jesus Christ. Induced from biblical passages such as Matt. 4:14, Swaggart argued that Christ

---

[48]Swaggart, "Our Upcoming Telethon," 31.
[49]Jimmy Swaggart, "From Me to You," *The Evangelist*, May/June 1991, 12.

promised to return only after every tribe and nation had heard the gospel. Since his program was the only program capable of fulfilling this prerequisite, one could conclude that Swaggart had been called to be the instrument by which the path for "D-Day," or Christ's literal, physical return to earth, would be laid. But if the people did not fulfill their part of God's calling and support the program, then Christ would delay his return. Thus, if the listener did not financially support Swaggart, then that listener was personally responsible for apocalyptic delay.

Some, no doubt, would respond that if Swaggart does not do it, then someone else would take his place in this grand scheme. In an earlier message, however, Swaggart responded forcefully to such an objection:

> There is no one else who can carry out this effort. I must do it. God has called me to do it. He has laid His hand on my life to do it. As the great Paul was called to take the gospel to the Gentile world, I have been called to reach the masses with the gospel of Jesus Christ as well. If you think there are many others out there—or even one other person—who can do it, you are so sadly mistaken. I would to God that it were so. I wish there were thousands who could do it, but I know they aren't there. So if I do not do it, it will not be done. I know that to be the truth.[50]

Swaggart reminded his audience of his place in eschatological developments during his scandal campaign. By implication, every time he reminded them of his preeminence as an evangelist, he was invoking their memory of the D-Day prophecy. But even more directly, in one letter sent to contributors, he referred to yet another dream in which God told him to take the Gospel to "every available station in the world."[51] In another article in *The Evangelist*, Swaggart reminded his

---

[50]Swaggart, "Our Upcoming Telethon," 32.
[51]Swaggart, quoted in Case and Cutbirth, 14.

readers that he first received such a vision on July 1, 1985;[52] the vision to which he referred in his initial announcement of his "D-Day or Delay" program.

Such an argument was exceedingly effective for Swaggart's audience, driven as they were by premillennial beliefs and the view that the last times were imminent. If Christ is returning as soon as these prerequisites are met, then they had better be sure that they were supporting God's plan. After all, as Swaggart reminded his audience, "these are God's priorities, because these are the last days."[53]

The Work of the Prince of Darkness (Satan)

The subject of Satan surfaced a significant number of times during Swaggart's rhetorical campaign. At various times, he argued that

. . . it is Satan's business to do everything within his power to stop this which God is doing.[54]

Satan has been trying to destroy me with a terrible problem.[55]

I think you would understand that a terrible tragedy of this nature would hurt the Ministry—and this is exactly what Satan wanted.[56]

In the last few weeks Satan has pressed his hand down strong to destroy these ministries.[57]

---

[52]Swaggart, "God's Priorities," 10.
[53]Ibid.
[54]Swaggart, "Our Upcoming Telethon," 31.
[55]Swaggart, "A Personal Message," 1.
[56]Swaggart, "A Personal Message," 1.
[57]These words were spoken by Frances during the telethon. See "Swaggart's Wife," A6.

. . . it is fairly obvious that the devil tried to destroy this ministry.[58]

The program will go off the air without additional support. That's what Satan wants; is that what you want?[59]

Guilt is one of Satan's greatest weapons. It is so severe that vocabulary cannot describe it. (see Appendix B).

Grounds ------------>	Warrants ------------->	Minor Claims ---------->Major Claims	
Satan has tried everything to destroy me and this ministry.	"Your adversary, the devil, prowls about like a roaring lion, seeking someone to devour." (I Pet. 5:8) Implied: Satan reserves his severest attacks for those who do the most for God.	The severity of Satan's attack upon me is evidence that I am doing great things for God. To remove me from ministry is to give Satan a victory against his fiercest rival.	I am worthy of forgiveness and continued support.

Based upon these arguments that Satan tried to destroy the Swaggart ministries, the evangelist implied that Satan's reason for doing so was the ministries' effectiveness in doing God's bidding. Virtually every reference to Satan is preceded or followed by a recounting of the recent successes of the ministry in the task of world evangelism. Considering that this struggle with Satan is often referred to as a battle, it follows that the first goal of Satan must be to neutralize those enemies who are enjoying the greatest gains. One follower mentioned

---

[58]Swaggart, quoted in Case and Cutbirth, 18.
[59]Swaggart, quoted in Case and Cutbirth, 26.

as much when he remarked to a visiting reporter, "He must have been doing something right because the devil's really working on him."[60]

Swaggart was not the first Pentecostal icon to defend himself from scandal accusations with this line of reasoning. In fact, at least two other equally well-known ministers used a much more direct form of this argument. In 1922, flamboyant evangelist Aimee Semple McPherson was accused by the press of faking her own kidnaping so that she could have an romantic affair. During her first Sunday back from her disappearance, she staged an elaborate drama, in which two demons discussed how they might destroy McPherson, who was clearly "their most crippling foe in Los Angeles."[61] Satan himself finally descended to inform his demon cohorts that he has decided to use the rumors of scandal to bring McPherson down.

A little over sixty years later, Jim Bakker used a similar argument. Shortly after the reports surfaced of his affair with Jessica Hahn, Bakker spoke these words:

> And who does he attack the most? Why, those who are doing the most, of course! If you're not causing him a problem, he leaves you alone. But if you are making a positive impact for Christ in the lives of thousands, if you are faithfully and consistently doing the will of God, if you are devoting all of your time and energies to tearing down the forces of evil—then it is you that he must attack with all of his might.[62]

If one accepts these warrants and the legitimacy of their grounds, the claims logically follow: the reality of the attack is evidence of the effectiveness of the rhetor, and to refuse the rhetor forgiveness is to participate in Satan's grand conspiracy to destroy the ministry. This is

---

[60]Amy Wilson, "Jimmy Swaggart: The Forgiven," *Ft. Lauderdale Sun-Sentinel,* 12 March 1989, 5E.

[61]Robert Bahr, *Least of All Saints: The Story of Aimee Semple McPherson* (Englewood Cliffs: Prentice, 1979), 232.

[62]Jim Bakker, *The PTL Club,* 12 December 1987, Channel 38, Chicago, IL.

a group who knew about conspiracies (as will be explained in the next chapter), and this is one conspiracy they will not want any part of.

Demon Possession

The only time that Swaggart specifically mentioned the notion of demons during his rhetorical campaign was in his final letter to his followers during his preaching layoff. Swaggart stated that "an attack of demonic forces of darkness became so severe that I really do not have

Grounds ------------>	Warrants ------------>	Minor Claims ---------->	Major Claims
I was possessed by the demon of lust.	Implied: Demon possession is not a voluntary condition.	I was not responsible for what I did.	I am worthy of forgiveness and continued support.
The demon was exorcised from my body.			

the words to convey to you what actually happened."[63] But weeks earlier, through limited access media,[64] Swaggart's audience was told of a secret exorcism performed on Swaggart by fellow televangelist Oral Roberts. Roberts contacted Swaggart after observing "demons with long fingernails digging into the flesh of Jimmy Swaggart's body."[65] Roberts exorcised the demons and Swaggart is reported to have told his close associates that Roberts "freed him from the demonic influences that caused his misbehavior."[66]

The belief in demon possession and oppression is widespread among Pentecostal audiences. Poloma reports that eighty-six percent of

---

[63]Swaggart, quoted in Case and Cutbirth, 20.
[64]See Chapter 3, footnote 35.
[65]Milam (Newsbank: E13).
[66]Ibid.

Assembly of God pastors reported having prayed for deliverance from demon oppression during a church service.[67] It is likely that virtually all faithful Pentecostals believe in demons and in demon possession, for emphasis upon an unseen Holy Spirit naturally aligns with a belief in equally unseen unholy spirits.

No one biblical passage provided Swaggart and his doctrinal community with the ammunition necessary for arguing that demon oppression is involuntary. But a forced invasion is consistent with the New Testament narratives that detail a demon possession.[68] In addition, the words used to describe such an act: "attacked," "possessed," clearly suggest that the victim of these forces of darkness may not be able to do anything to resist them.

Interestingly, this notion of demon oppression became even more prominent when Swaggart is caught with a second prostitute in 1991. As will be explained in chapter six, Swaggart argued that an entire legion of demons descended upon him with such power that, once again, not even he could defeat it.

Interpersonal Forgiveness Between Christians

By arguing that since God had forgiven him his audience should do likewise, Swaggart raised the issue of forgiveness. Confession of faults, however, went beyond the relationship between God and human beings. This community also teaches the necessity of confession within the community of faith. As the passage of James above suggests, Christians should confess their faults to one another. Thus when Swaggart wrote in his March 19 letter, "When I bared all to my brethren, that was the right thing to do,"[69] he was stating more than just the fact that he was honest; he was stating that he was following biblical mandates. Once again, these mandates were able to be successfully transformed into warrants for his arguments.

---

[67]Poloma, 85.

[68]For example, see the story of the two demoniacs in Matthew 8:28-34.

[69]Swaggart, "A Personal Message," 1.

Grounds --------------->	Warrants ------------>	Minor Claims ---------->Major Claims
I confessed my sin to you.	"Confess your sins to one another . . . that you may be healed." (James 5:16)	I have followed the procedure to secure your forgiveness.	I am worthy of forgiveness and continued support.

The Fontaines referred often to this "biblical pattern"[70] of public confession between Christians. In one section, they claim that if a believer follows this pattern, then fellow Christians have absolutely no options as to an appropriate response: "There may be a tendency to consider as optional whether or not to forgive him. It isn't. The Bible makes it clear that as part of our Christian walk, we must forgive him."[71] Thus, if Swaggart's audience believes the Bible, and if Swaggart followed the biblical guidelines for such a situation, then their response can only be to accede to Swaggart's major claim of forgiveness and continued support.

Intercessory Prayer

The grounds for this argument were subtly laid in his opening apology sermon. As Swaggart reflected upon the cause of his actions, he pondered, "I did not find the victory I sought because I did not seek the help of my brothers and sisters in the Lord" (see Appendix A). Weeks later, however, in a section of *The Evangelist*, he made his grounds abundantly clear when he printed this letter he received from

---

[70]Fontaine, 6.
[71]Fontaine, 54.

Grounds ------------>	Warrants ------------->	Minor Claims ----------->	Major Claims
I fell into sin.	"Prayers, petitions and thanksgiving, be made on behalf of all men, for kings and all who are in authority..(I Tim. 2:1,2)

Implied: Without that intercessory prayer, a Christian leader cannot hope to win the spiritual battle. | My sin is actually the fault of those fellow Christians who failed to pray for me. | I am worthy of forgiveness and continued support. |

Assemblies of God missionary Mark Buntain. After Buntain admitted that he had failed Swaggart by not praying for his "life to be protected from the onslaught of Satan's power," Buntain continues:

> I am guilty. The whole Christian community is guilty, and we need to first ask God to forgive us and then ask you to forgive us. I promise you, it will never happen again.
> Brother Jimmy, the battle is not over but neither are you and neither are we. You are God's special man, and from now on we will not only be with you but we will be behind you, behind you and around you claiming the power of Jesus' precious blood to cover and keep you.[72]

---

[72]Mark Buntain, *The Evangelist*, June, 1988, quoted in Fontaine, 153.

Derived from the simple biblical admonition to pray for those in leadership over you, this letter suggests that a lack of this supporting prayer means that the prayer is the one to blame, not the leader who fell into sin.

Such an understanding endows the final words of the March 19 letter with added significance: "Lift up this ministry in prayer every day. These are certainly the most trying times we've ever faced and we need your prayers now more than ever."[73] By inference, if the needed support were not raised or if the ministry failed entirely, or even if Swaggart fell into sin a second time, then the fingers of blame need only point toward those who stood watching from the sidelines instead of being on their knees in prayer for Swaggart.

Through an analysis of shared doctrinal warrants, we have observed that what appeared to be an open and contrite confession of wrongdoing was actually anything but that. Through his use of shared beliefs, Swaggart blamed demons and even other Christians for his acts of weakness. He also suggested that a commitment to the Bible demands a quick restoration. Many of these same themes made up the underbelly of the stories that Jimmy Swaggart told to further his case.

---

[73]Swaggart, "A Personal Message," 2.

5

THE RESPONSE: STORYTELLING AS ARGUMENT

In their greed these teachers will exploit you with stories they have made up.
—2 Peter 2:3

THE FREQUENT USE OF STORYTELLING BY SWAGGART DID NOT BEGIN with his scandal defense. Because Swaggart is a religious rhetor, a Southern rhetor, and a television rhetor, narrative was bound to find its place near the center of his rhetorical world. Given that context, it is not surprising that Swaggart would make regular use of stories as he attempted to convince his audience that he was worthy of their forgiveness and continued support.

HOW STORIES WORK AS ARGUMENTS

Robert C. Rowland helpfully defines narrative as "essentially a chronological account of an event or process involving the formal characteristics of a plot and character development."[1] Further, we are interested in the genre of narrative that John Louis Lucaites and Celeste Michelle Condit term "rhetorical narrative."[2] Extending the Aristotelian and Quintillian notion of "*narratio*," define rhetorical narrative as a "story that serves as an interpretive lens through which the audience is asked to view and understand the verisimilitude of the propositions and

---

[1] Robert C. Rowland, "Narrative: Mode of Discourse or Paradigm?" *Communication Monographs* 54 (September 1987): 267.
[2] John Louis Lucaites and Celeste Michelle Condit, "Re-Constructing Narrative Theory: A Functional Perspective," *Journal of Communication* 35 (1985):94.

proof before it."[3] Unlike poetic and dialectical narrative, Lucaites and Condit explain that "both content and form of the rhetorical narrative are thus subservient to the demands of the relationship between the specific audience to which it is addressed, the specific context in which it appears, and the specific gain toward which it strives."[4]

Lucaites and Condit extend their view of rhetorical narrative by explaining that these stories tend to share two additional characteristics: brevity and consistency.[5] In terms of brevity, they explain that since rhetorical narratives are posited to accomplish a specific rhetorical purpose, rhetors rarely bore or distract their listeners with inconsequential details. Instead, users of rhetorical narratives tend to focus the attention towards only the most central issues. In addition, rhetorical narrative users can rely upon their audiences to fill in many of the missing details, since the narratives were chosen and crafted with the audience's knowledge base in mind. This is not to suggest that rhetorical narratives do not take advantage of the power of detail to captivate attention; it is only to suggest that of all genres of narrative, rhetorical narratives will be the most likely to exclude what may seem to be extraneous details.

In terms of consistency, Lucaites and Condit emphasize that, unlike poetic and dialectic narratives, rhetorical narratives are crafted to be consistent with situational and audience expectations and world views. Although all narratives carry a burden to display consistency, rhetorical narratives tend to have a much more heightened sensitivity to situational and audience-related issues.

The effectiveness of narrative as a tool of argument is generally undisputed by rhetorical scholars. The reasons for this unanimity of opinion were the subject of considerable reflection on the part of Roderick P. Hart. Hart argues that narrative succeeds as argument for at least five reasons.

First, narrative does not argue in *obvious* ways. Hart suggests:

---

[3]Lucaites and Condit 94.
[4]Ibid.
[5]Ibid, 96-98.

If a narrator tries to make a point too forcefully, we feel cheated. Good narrative holds open the illusion that we—as listeners and readers—help to determine its meaning. Narrative is depropositionalized argument, argument with a hidden bottom line. Narrators charm audiences because they only promise a story well told.[6]

Irving Rein, Philip Kotler, and Martin Stoller support Hart's claim by applying Don Idhe's philosophy of communication delivery systems to storytelling.[7] Idhe argues that the more transparent a message delivery system is, the less its imperfections interfere with its use, and the less one is aware of the way that the technology alters the communication process. In the same way, narrative works because it does not *appear* to be an argument. Listeners are less cognitively aware of the "message delivery system," and thus are less likely, in the language of persuasion research, to process the argument centrally.

This entire project is devoted to looking at Swaggart's reasoning, with an emphasis on those arguments that did not appear to be arguments. Hart's analysis tells us that an argument embraced in the arms of a narrative tends to seduce auditors by appearing to be something other than what it really is.

Second, narrative occurs in a natural time-line. Hart notes, "There are beginnings, middles, and endings to narrative. Once we start on a narrative, we feel compelled to follow it through to its conclusion. All stories, even bad stories, inspire the need to see how they turn out. Narratives always tempt us with closure."[8]

This notion is compatible with Kenneth Burke's concept of the psychology of form. Burke defined form as "an arousing and fulfillment of desires," and "the creation of an appetite in the mind of the auditor,

---

[6]Roderick P. Hart, *Modern,* 133.

[7]Irving Rein, Philip Kotler, and Martin Stoller, *High Visibility* (New York: Dodd, 1987), 148.

[8]Roderick P. Hart, *Modern,* 133.

and the adequate satisfying of that appetite."[9] For example, just as a syllogistic progression prepares the reader to expect the next line of argument, or a sonnet causes the listener to expect the lines given in a certain rhyme, so a narrative causes a listener to want to stay for the climax and anticlimax. Thus, the mere beginning of the journey causes in the listener a desire to know what lies at the end of the road.

In some ways, Swaggart's entire ordeal is a narrative that produced a desire to wait for the final outcome. When Swaggart proclaims "the best is yet to come,"[10] the listener cannot help but to be motivated to consider how this real-life story will turn out. But along the way, Swaggart offered self-contained stories that produced equally compelling reasons for listeners to stay until the journey's end.

Third, narrative includes characterization. Again Hart writes: "People are interested in people. Narratives are the stories of what people do. Often, narratives introduce interesting people, sometimes grand people, to an audience. When we read or hear such narratives, our natural sense of identification makes us want to find out more about the lives of the people described."[11]

Once again, one of Burke's key concepts adds support to Hart's claim. Burke argued that all persuasion is accomplished as a result of identification: "You persuade a man only insofar as you can talk his language by speech, gesture, tonality, order, image, attitude, idea, identifying your ways with his."[12] To the extent that a listener identifies with the characters of a story, that story possesses power to influence the listener.

The fact that rhetorical narrative offers less detail about the characters it introduces does not deny it the power of identification. As explained above, audiences often possess within their memory the characters and their characteristics. Just because the rhetor does not

---

[9]Kenneth Burke, *Counter-Statement* (Berkeley: University of California Press, 1931) .

[10]Swaggart, quoted in Dunne, "Evangelist Says" (Newsbank: E12).

[11]Roderick P. Hart, *Modern,* 133.

[12]Kenneth Burke, *A Rhetoric of Motives* (Berkeley: University of California Press, 1969), 21.

mention them does not mean that they do not live in the mind of the listener.

Fourth, narrative presents detail. Again Hart writes: "A good story, such as a fine novel, transports us into another time or place by offering fine-grained treatments. When the narrator describes the clothes people wear or the customs they follow or the dialect they speak, we come to know that time and place as if it were our own. Details captivate."[13]

Again, rhetorical narratives do this with the help of the listener. Lucaites and Condit offer an example of a speaker who makes an elusive reference to "Watergate."[14] Although no details may be verbalized by the rhetor, due to the shared knowledge and understanding between rhetor and audience, the audience is capable of filling in most of the detail for themselves.

Fifth, narrative is primitive. "No culture exists without narrative. Most cultures celebrate their sacred narratives on a regular basis (for example, a Fourth of July celebration) and indoctrinate their young by means of narrative (for example, fairy tales). Narrative appeals to the child in us, because, unlike life, it contains a complete story with certain consequences."[15]

Ernest G. Borhmann's symbolic convergence theory provides strong support for Hart's final observation. Bohrman argued that his theory explained the "appearance of a group consciousness, with its implied shared emotions, motives, and meanings, not in terms of individual daydreams and scripts but rather in terms of socially shared narrations or fantasies."[16] As will be demonstrated in the narrative analysis section, many of these stories can be found throughout other ages and other contexts, for they have a history of being used to uphold the shared fantasies, beliefs, and values of their cultural adherents.

In sum, narratives not only should be considered as argument, but in many situations, they may be the most powerful of all arguments. As

---

[13]Roderick P. Hart, *Modern,* 133.

[14]Lucaites and Condit, 96.

[15]Roderick P. Hart, *Modern,* 133.

[16]Ernest G. Bormann, "Symbolic Convergence Theory: A Communication Formulation," *Journal of Communication* 35.4 (Autumn, 1985): 128.

Kathleen Hall Jamieson explains: "The dramatic tale has more power to involve and to propel that leap (from anecdote to generalized assertion) than do the statistics that would better warrant that claim . . . if a trusted speaker tells the story with conviction, we suspend disbelief."[17]

Although some of Hart's reasons for the persuasive power of narrative generally fall outside the realm of rational proof, audiences still judge narrative reasoning as rationally compelling. To discern how those judgments are arrived at through the audiences' previous beliefs and values, we once again turn to Toulmin's model for unpacking informal argument. Toulmin's model is an appropriate way to dissect rhetorical narratives for three reasons. First, although they are depropositionalized, they do, as Hart explains, have a "hidden bottom line."[18] In Toulmin's terms, they are arguments with hidden but very real *claims*. Second, as arguments, they are crafted with a particular audience in mind and they are completed with the help of that audience. Toulmin argues that they rely upon shared *warrants* between speaker and audience. Third, both in form and in substance, they do provide reasons or *grounds* for agreeing with the rhetor's goals.

In light of these reasons, we turn again to Toulmin's model to aid in the deconstruction of Swaggart's stories. The result may be, as Rowland ponders in a separate but related context, that "such an analysis might strip the film of aesthetic appeal, but the analysis would get at the film's argumentative quality."[19]

---

[17]Kathleen Hall Jamieson, *Eloquence in an Electronic Age* (New York: Oxford University Press, 1988), 152.

[18]Hart, *Modern*, 133.

[19]Robert C. Rowland, "The Value of the Rational World and Narrative Paradigms," *Central States Speech Journal* 39/3 & 4 (Fall/Winter 1988): 208.

SWAGGART'S NARRATIVE ARGUMENTS

Great Rivalry[20]

Swaggart spoke much about his adversarial relationship with the ultimate enemy—Satan. As a result of Satan's anger over the success of Swaggart's ministry, Satan and his army of demons made Swaggart a target of constant attack. Swaggart referred to his battles often, but his

Grounds ------------>	Warrants ---------->	Minor Claims ---------->	Major Claims
I have been engaged in battle against a fierce and terrible adversary.	God reveals truth through dreams. The Leviathan is Satan himself —the ultimate adversary. The man in the shadows is the Lord himself. Satan attacks hardest those that are doing the most for God.	I am not responsible for what has happened.	I am worthy of forgiveness and continued support.

adversarial struggles found their most dramatic expression in the opening moments of his comeback sermon:

---

[20]Rein, 152. Examples cited by the authors of this story line are Joe Louis and Max Schmeling; Jack Benny and Fred Allen; Picasso and Braque; Bjorn Borg and John McEnroe; Greg LeMond and Bernard Hinault; Michael DeBakey and Denton Cooley.

A year and a half ago I had two dreams. . . . I dreamed I was in a church. The church was empty; it was not this one, and I was tied or held down to the floor flat on my back against the far wall. I remember wanting to get to the platform, to the pulpit, but I could not. . . . In the aisle where I was spread eagle on my back on the floor, unable to get up; the aisle ran vertical and in that aisle was the largest serpent that I had ever seen up to then. It must have stretched a hundred feet long. I must have been four, five, six feet tall and it stretched the entire length of the church from me to the platform and the pulpit. I did not know what it meant. . . . And that same night, I had a similar dream. I, with a sword or a club, I do not remember which, was in a house and I was fighting a serpent. It was large and it attacked me standing as tall as I was and I was fighting the serpent and I remember the struggle was so intense. There was a man whom I did not know standing in the shadows. He was not evil because of the look on his face that I could see. He was watching me; he stood and looked without comment as I fought this thing, fighting with all the strength I had and I finally subdued it and killed it. . . . I was standing exhausted with this club in my hand, standing outside the house and I looked to my right. I thought at first it was a huge concrete pillar standing a hundred or so feet high, but then it moved, and when it moved it felt like the earth was shaking and I looked and I saw it was another serpent. Much larger than the one I mentioned a moment ago. It seemed to stand, as I said, a hundred feet or more high, its head darting about, its body as large, almost, as this octagon. . . . And the thing moved and the ground shook. And I remember my knees buckling and I awakened from the dream looking up at it, saying "God, I have to fight this and I don't know how to do it. How can I over-come this huge Leviathan?" (see Appendix B)

In response to prayers offered to God through "sobbing and literally doubled-up weeping," Swaggart told his audience that God had revealed the purpose and meaning of the dreams by giving him the answers he sought. God revealed that this was one battle that Swaggart could not win alone. But God himself could win the battle, by merely saying, "Satan I rebuke thee. And he is defeated." Thus, Swaggart, a mighty warrior who had successfully battled his adversary for years, finally came upon the weapon of the enemy he could not subdue alone. Fortunately for Swaggart, his commander-in-chief was able and willing to take over just in the nick of time.

There is one interesting subplot of the dream for which Swaggart does not offer an interpretation, but whose meaning his audience was no doubt able to discern. At one point, Swaggart mentioned that he was "held down" on the floor, unable to get to the pulpit. His audience would be well aware that the only person or thing preventing him from getting to the pulpit was the Assemblies of God council. So, in this dream, Swaggart argues that the denominational hierarchy was working on the side of the great adversary.

Shared belief in the veracity of many of the warrants was established in chapter four. In terms of belief in the spiritual utility of dreams, Swaggart's primary audience would lean on verses such as Matt. 2:13, an "angel of the Lord appeared to Joseph in a dream," for support that dreams communicate the truths of God. Also, Swaggart listed dreams as one of the seven ways that God communicated to man today.[21]

Apart from this dream narrative, Swaggart's references to the great rivalry story line displayed the rhetorical narrative characteristics of brevity and consistency. The audience knew how to fill in the blanks, for they had come to understand the warlike position that all Christians were in as they attempted to battle Satan and his forces. Swaggart graphically illustrated this warlike stance during one of his earlier sermons, which he entitled "If the Foundations Be Destroyed":

We're gonna turn it around, with God's help we're gonna turn it around. I want to serve notice on you—we Christians, born

---

[21]Swaggart, *Straight Answers,* 169.

again, are declaring war! We are declaring war on the monkeys in our classrooms; we are declaring war upon the secular humanists; we are declaring war on the atheists and evolutionists; we are declaring war on the abortionists. We're bringing back the Bible to the United States of America.[22]

The dream and other rivalry/adversary narratives reminded Swaggart's audience that a warrior ought not be blamed for losing an occasional battle to a tough enemy, especially in light of his many earlier successes. After all, the first leviathan lay dead on the floor, the victim of Swaggart's considerable warrior-like skills.

The "Virtuous" Fatal Flaw[23]

Based upon the examples given by Rein, Kotler, and Stoller, the version of the "fatal flaw" narrative used by Swaggart is actually a subset

Grounds --------> Warrants ----------> Minor Claims ----------> Major Claims			
I devoted every waking moment to the cause of world evangelism.	A cause and effect relationship existed between Swaggart's compassion, devotion, ministry efforts, and his sin.	The causes of my sin were actually to be praised.	I am worthy of forgiveness and continued support.
I worked myself to utter exhaustion for the sake of the ministry.			

---

[22]Swaggart, quoted in Harvey, 98.

[23]The authors of *High Visibility* speak only of a "Fatal Flaw" story line (152), and as explained in the discourse above, I am exploring a specific subset of that particular narrative. In terms of the general story line, the authors cite the examples of Ted Kennedy and morality; Jimmy Piersall and depression; Janis Joplin and drugs; Richard Nixon and paranoia; Vanessa Williams and indiscretion.

of the general narrative. In *High Visibility*, most of the examples were stories of famous men and women who lost their fame or position by succumbing to that one weakness, that one vice they could not resist. Although that could certainly be applied to Swaggart, he weaves a fatal flaw story line that ran in a slightly different direction. In this story line, the hero falls due to his or her commitment to a virtue or virtuous act. For example, when questioned about his behavior the night of the murder of Mary Jo Kopechne, Senator Ted Kennedy referred to his repeated heroic attempts at saving Miss Kopechne as the reasons for his irrational behavior. President Reagan, when responding to allegations that he traded arms for hostages, remarked that his greatest flaw was that he tended to trust those who worked for him. Similarly, Swaggart spoke of the causes of his sin as simply that he cared too much and worked too hard for the ministry.

At first it might appear that the *virtuous* fatal flaw narrative is similar to the transcendence strategy in apologia, where the accused denies wrongdoing because he or she was obeying a higher cause or higher authority. However, in the examples of the virtuous fatal flaw, the accused admits wrongdoing, but hopes that the audience will accept that the value behind the cause of the wrongdoing outweighs the transgression itself. Thus, absolution is the only appropriate response.

Grounds for this narrative can be found in the leviathan dream analyzed above. Recall that after successfully slaying the first serpent, Swaggart found that he had been fighting with "all the strength that I had." In addition to this reference, Swaggart mentions in the March 19 letter: "For some time, Frances and I worked to the point of total exhaustion, and possibly we did not use wisdom in doing this thing. But the urgency of the message and the magnitude of the Ministry itself have driven us many times beyond our strength."[24]

In the April edition of *The Evangelist*, Swaggart proclaimed:

We have tried to carry the load of a thousand men. Both Frances and I have buckled under it. I do not blame anyone for

---

[24]Swaggart, "A Personal Message," 1.

the past mistakes except Jimmy Swaggart, but I do know when one works from total exhaustion week after week and month after month, there will be a breakdown of some kind. Most of the time it is physical; some of the time it is spiritual. Strangely enough, I did not break down physically or spiritually. It came in another direction.[25]

Swaggart's message was that although he may have committed a sin, in light of the mammoth load that he carried for the Kingdom of Christ, such a breakdown was to be expected.

In some ways, this argument parallels the reasoning of the doctrine of Satan arguments. In that line of reasoning, Swaggart's fall was evidence of his prominence in God's economy since Satan works hardest on God's best workers. Similarly, Swaggart's fall is an indication of the effort he was putting into building the Kingdom of God, for certainly he never would have fallen had it not been for the fact that he was carrying the load of "a thousand men."

Success/Adversity/Success[26]

The evening news, weekly docudramas, and tabloids are full of stories of famous individuals who fall out of favor with the public, only to fight their way back to the top.[27] It was no different in biblical times, and Swaggart calls upon those stories to strengthen his case for restoration.

Swaggart first invoked the Old Testament story of David.[28] David was the King of Israel when he spied Bathsheba, the beautiful wife of Uriah the Hittite, bathing on a house top near the palace. After committing adultery with Bathsheba, David arranged to have Uriah

---

[25]Swaggart, "I Just Want," 12.

[26]Rein, 152. Examples cited by the authors are Mickey Rooney; Pierre Trudeau; Judy Garland; Bob Dylan; Tina Turner; Freddie Laker; Tommy John.

[27]In addition to the examples mentioned by the authors, more recent examples would include Cher, Alice Cooper, and Jerry Brown.

[28]The story is found in 2 Sam. 11, 12.

killed in battle. Once his sin was discovered, David repented, but not before he lost his son as punishment. Eventually, David regained his

Grounds --------- ->	Warrants ----------->	Minor Claims --------->	Major Claims
Peter experienced spiritual success, then scandal, and then his greatest success.	My situation is analogous to Peter's and David's.	If God can use these men after moral failure, he can use me.	I am worthy of forgiveness and continued support.
David experienced spiritual success, then scandal, and then his greatest success.			

previous position. In fact, in spite of his atrocious deeds, David was gloriously labeled "a man after God's own heart (I Sam. 13:14)."

Swaggart's first reference to David occurred in the conclusion of his apology sermon. Swaggart prefaced a biblical passage he intended to read with "I close this today with the words of another man that lived 3,000 years ago—and I started to say who committed sin worse than mine, but I take that back. And if the Holy Spirit will allow me to borrow his words. . . ." (see Appendix A) Swaggart then recited the confessional prayer of David that he prayed after his adulterous affair with Bathsheba. Although Swaggart offered no details or background to the prayer, his audience was no doubt able to fill in the background of the narrative.

Swaggart again made reference to David in the April 1988 issue of *The Evangelist*. Swaggart's column "The Word for Every Day," dealt with David and the people's unwillingness to follow him during his times of trial.[29] According to Swaggart, David learned that trials eventually bring increased blessing and faith, and he learned that even when all those who supported you are missing, God still stays and still cares for his own. In this case, the parallels are too obvious to be missed by anyone.

A third reference to David was found in the May Actiongram that was sent to supporters. Swaggart clearly reminded his readers of the details of the David story, such as the murder and his subsequent forgiveness.[30]

Incidentally, there was at least one other similarity between David and Swaggart that stems from a lesser known moment in the David story. Consequently, his audience may not be aware of it, and Swaggart was content to keep it that way. After the affair with Bathsheba and the murder of Uriah, the prophet Nathan came to David with the following situation for judgment:

> There were two men in one city, the one rich and the other poor. The rich man had a great many flocks and herds. But the poor man had nothing except one little ewe lamb, which he bought and nourished; and it grew up together with him and his children. It would eat of his bread and drink of his cup and lie in his bosom, and was like a daughter to him.
>
> Now a traveler came to the rich man, and he was unwilling to take from his own herd, to prepare for the wayfarer who had come to him; rather, he took the poor man's ewe lamb and prepared it for the man who had come to him (I Sam. 12: 1-4).

The passage declares that David in anger condemned the rich man to death for his selfishness. At that moment, Nathan dramatically turned towards David with the words, "You are that man (I Sam. 12:7)!" Interestingly, this is strikingly similar to the many pronouncements of judgment that Swaggart made concerning Bakker and others

---

[29]Swaggart, "The Word," 10.
[30]Swaggart, quoted in Case and Cutbirth, 16.

during their scandals. Swaggart was also asked to judge the actions of others—actions that he himself had already committed. But the difference was that David was willing to accept a harsh punishment for his transgression. Swaggart, on the other hand, had what the Fontaines referred to as a simple case of "changing his mind."[31]

Swaggart next turned to the New Testament for his story line. The Apostle Peter's moment of weakness found him denying his association with Christ just prior to Jesus' arrest. Peter eventually repented and goes on to further the cause of Christianity throughout the region, including his conversion of three thousand pagans just fifty days after his denial of knowing Christ.

At least two of Swaggart's rhetorical references to the Peter narrative were more overt than his use of David. In the May edition of *The Evangelist*, Swaggart reminded his readers that "some fifty days following Peter's denial, he was preaching on the Day of Pentecost—and we know that three thousand were saved."[32] Swaggart was equally brazen when he offered his repentance paradigm that we discussed in chapter four. He argued that the Peter story demonstrated that if a Christian had repented from his sin and if he had demonstrated Holy Spirit involvement in his life and ministry after his repentance, then that repentance was genuine.

Swaggart's other references to Peter were more subtle. On at least two occasions, he made use of the Peter narrative when he described, also in narrative form, of hearing God cry out to Swaggart, "Feed my sheep!"[33] This referred to Peter's call to world evangelism in John 21:15-17. On one other occasion, Swaggart proclaimed that as "Peter was called to the Jews. . . . I have been called to perform a specific work at a specific moment in time."[34] Since his audience would know that Peter performed this task subsequent to his moral failure, then no doubt Swaggart should be afforded the same opportunity.

---

[31]Fontaine, 55.
[32]Dunne, "Swaggart to Oversee," (Newsbank: E8).
[33]Swaggart, "A Personal," 1; Swaggart, "I Just Want to Say," 12.
[34]Swaggart, "God's Priorities," 10.

Did Swaggart's audience accept these parallels between Swaggart and David and Peter? There are at least two anecdotal pieces of evidence that suggest they did. The Fontaines devoted an entire chapter to "Peter: An Example."[35] In this chapter, the authors point out that Peter's call must have been irrevocable because his greatest success occurred after his fall. They then go on to hypothesize that if Peter had been an Assembly of God minister, the evangelistic harvest that occurred on the day of Pentecost may have been prevented by the unbiblical actions of the Assemblies of God Presbytery.

In a message Swaggart preached a few months after his comeback, one supporter told a reporter that to understand why he is still supporting Swaggart, "Let's look at David."[36] He went on to point out the parallels between David's fall and subsequent glory, and his own.

Perhaps a key reason for believing that Swaggart's audience would accept this argument is that they had a rather powerful motive for doing so. By accepting the parallel between the David and Peter narratives and the Swaggart situation, they were affirming that the Bible was relevant for today. God not only used fallen and broken persons in biblical times, but still used them in 1988. A vote in favor of Swaggart was a vote in favor of the veracity and continued relevance of the Bible.

Stand by Your Man

Frances Swaggart, Jimmy's wife, played a prominent role in the rhetorical campaign of 1988. In the apology sermon, Frances received the first of the pleas for forgiveness from the quivering lips of her sorrowful husband. After addressing a few comments to the press, Swaggart turned around to face his wife, who was seated on the platform behind him. In a hushed voice, Swaggart began:

---

[35]Fontaine, 35-37.
[36]Wilson 5E.

First of all, my wife, Frances—God never gave a man a better helpmate and companion to stand beside him. And as far as this gospel has been taken through the airwaves to the great cities of the world and covered this globe, it would never have been done were it not for her strength, her courage, her consecration to her Redeemer, the Lord Jesus Christ. I have sinned against you. And I beg your forgiveness (see Appendix A).

Grounds ---------->	Warrants ------------>	Minor Claims ---------->	Major Claims
My wife has forgiven me.	She has the greatest motivation not to forgive me.	If she has forgiven me, then so should you.	I am worthy of forgiveness and continued support.

During the initial portion of these statements, the television camera focused on Swaggart's tortured expression as he struggled to get out the words in a trembling voice. But as his plea reached its conclusion, the cameras showed a subdued Frances, who merely offered a nod of approval at her husband's request for forgiveness.[37] Just one week later, Frances was prominently involved in three segments of the comeback campaign. In the letter sent to supporters on the March 19, Swaggart mentioned that "the moment I told Frances of this problem, I sensed victory."[38] That same week, Frances led the telethon to save the ministry that Satan was attempting to destroy.[39] Finally, in the April issue of *The Evangelist*, Jimmy and Frances penned a letter entitled, "I Just Want to Say, 'We Love You.'" In the letter, Frances is quoted as saying, "for the

---

[37]According to televangelist critic Quentin Schultze, a number of sources told him that Frances did not want to attend the service. Furious at the news of his actions, Frances did not want anything to do with her husband. But according to Schultze's sources, Swaggart convinced Frances that it would be best for both of them if she attended. Quentin Schultze, telephone interview, 12 Feb. 1993.

[38]Swaggart, "A Personal Message," 1.

[39]"Swaggart's Wife," A6.

last two or three years it seems we heard steadily from our enemies (as well as our friends), but for the past several weeks, we have heard only from our friends."[40] There were other references to her and by her throughout the campaign, but one of her most significant contributions came in the final stage of the campaign—the comeback sermon. Before Jimmy rose to speak, Frances spoke for five minutes, delivering the following comments:

> You know we have lived for the Lord Jesus many, many years but yet never has He been as real and as close as He has been these past few months. . . . And there have been many dark nights and there have been many dark days but there have always been the bright times. . . . Our heart, our burden, and our souls are for the work of the Lord Jesus Christ. To be able to stand before you and tell you about Jesus and minister to you means more than . . . it's our heart and I thank God for that privilege that He has given me (see Appendix B).

From all appearances, Frances had forgiven her husband for his transgressions. Indeed, if the woman he most directly wronged by his deed forgave him, then what right would anyone else possess not to do the same? As with most of the stories Swaggart used, this one had doctrinal undertones. Not only did Swaggart's audience strongly believe in the principle that a wife should be in submission to her husband,[41] but this audience believed that there were no justified grounds for divorce. Swaggart explains:

> Among Christians, there are no grounds for divorce. . . . Many times Christians, because of weakness or temptation, fall into

---

[40]Swaggart, Jimmy and Frances, "I Just Want," 12.

[41]In *Straight Answers to Tough Questions*, Swaggart tackles the issue of submission of wives to husbands. He says: "The husband is to be the head of the home. He is to rule over it and preside over it, protecting it in love." (214) Swaggart goes on to suggest that a woman is to be obedient to her husband unless he asks her to do something immoral or illegal (216).

the sin of adultery. What then? If such a situation should occur (and sadly such situations occur all the time), the offending party should beg forgiveness from their spouse and from God. . . . Who can resist a repentant heart? . . . God promises He will not withhold forgiveness from anyone exhibiting a contrite heart. How can we?[42]

Clearly, Frances was not only repeating a centuries old moral drama of the wife who stands by her husband through hard and sometimes bitter circumstances, but she was obeying the commands of her truth source, at least as those commands were interpreted by her husband, as well as by those who share his world view.

The Conspiracy

During a sermon preached the week of his return to the pulpit, Swaggart had this to say:

I am certainly aware, as I am absolutely positive that all of you are, of the things that have been portrayed over television, in the papers. I have only seen a small part of it. However, I will say one thing. This alone. There are some very—and a lot of people . . . in this country—some very powerful, but very determined, to destroy this preacher, using any method at their disposal to do so. The pornographers are one of them, and the only thing I'll say . . . just don't believe everything you read, see, or hear.[43]

Swaggart gave no proof that the pornography industry had orchestrated his downfall, but this was an audience that probably needed little evidence to accept that the leaders of this demonic industry were behind

---

[42]Swaggart, *Straight Answers,* 243.

[43]Swaggart, quoted in Angela Simoneaux, "Swaggart Tells Crowd He's Healed," *Baton Rouge Morning Advocate* 26 May 1988 (Newsbank SOC file 53: E9).

Grounds ---------->	Warrants ---------->	Minor Claims ----------->	Major Claims
The pornographers were behind the accusations against me.	The porngraphers had something to gain by my downfall. The pornographers were capable of orchestrating my downfall. The porno graphers are evil men who would stoop to deception to bring Swaggart down.	You should not believe everything that you hear.	I am worthy of forgiveness and continued support.

any evil plan. This was true first because the mere nature of a conspiracy narrative accounted for a lack of supporting evidence. The less supporting evidence there is, the more successfully the conspiracy is keeping its deeds secret. For example, Hitler used this same reasoning to "prove" the existence of a Jewish banking conspiracy. To those who argued that there was no proof of such a conspiracy, Hitler responded that the absence of proof was evidence of how successful the Jews were in keeping their plan a secret.

A second and more substantive reason that Swaggart's primary audience would have little trouble believing that the pornographers were behind this was that Swaggart's doctrinal community spent much time talking about the evils of this industry. Not only was pornography one of Swaggart's favorite sermon topics, but the topic also found its way into many of his books. His two most popular books, *Rape of a Nation* and *Straight Answers to Tough Questions* both carry substantive sections on the topic of pornography. Interestingly, this narrative did not surface until late in the rhetorical campaign. The reason was probably due to the rhetorical situation in which Swaggart found himself at the time. In light of the public's disillusionment with the denial strategies of Bakker and others accused of wrongdoing, a blatant attempt at denial such as using the pornographers' conspiracy narrative would receive a great amount of negative publicity and reaction. But once things had settled down, and once Swaggart was primarily addressing his own doctrinal community, then there was no reason to avoid picking on one of this audiences' favorite targets.

The Underdog

On at least two occasions, Swaggart offered bits and pieces of a standard underdog narrative. On the day of his comeback sermon, Swaggart made a straightforward reference to this narrative: "I believe it is kind of hard to conceive of Jimmy Swaggart as the underdog, but that's what I am now. And Americans ally to an underdog."[44] But on

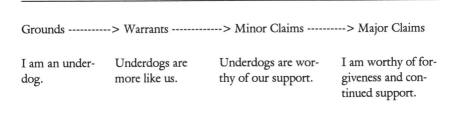

Grounds ---------->	Warrants ------------>	Minor Claims --------->	Major Claims
I am an underdog.	Underdogs are more like us.	Underdogs are worthy of our support.	I am worthy of forgiveness and continued support.

a second occasion, it was God himself who was part of the underdog role: "I truly believe, as the whole world looks on and says, 'It's impossible for that ministry to survive,' that God will bring it back so the world will have to say, 'God did it, for no man could do it.' "[45]

Once again, the airwaves are full of dramatic narratives of celebrities who overcome impossible odds to make it to the top. Many examples originate in the sports arena: Bo Jackson returning to the Chicago White Sox, despite hip replacement surgery; Jim Abbott pitching for

[44]Swaggart, quoted in Dunne, "Evangelist Says," (Newsbank: E13).
[45]Case and Cutbirth, 27.

the Angels and Yankees, despite being born with only one hand; and Wilma Rudolph becoming one of the premier track stars in the world, despite the fact that she contracted polio as a child. Even President Bill Clinton ran a campaign on the story line of the unlikely rise of a poor boy from the town of Hope, Arkansas. Perhaps the appeal of this narrative argument is that it affirms that our relative insignificance may one day be overcome. Perhaps one day we will rise higher than the expectations that others have for us.

Boy from Humble Beginnings

Swaggart's sermons are full of stories concerning his humble beginnings and struggling times. In addition, much of the first half of his autobiography retell the stories of a poor boy who struggled to make good.[46] When it came time for his campaign to salvage his empire, Swaggart turned to a very indirect representation of this story line. In the days following the scandal, Swaggart announced that he was

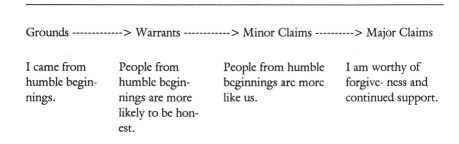

Grounds ------------>	Warrants ------------>	Minor Claims ---------->	Major Claims
I came from humble beginnings.	People from humble beginnings are more likely to be honest.	People from humble beginnings are more like us.	I am worthy of forgive- ness and continued support.

canceling most of his large international crusades, and he announced that he was planning a return to the sawdust trail in a series of crusades in rural and urban America. Although the crusades would not begin until after the rhetorical campaign was completed, the mere announcing of them conjured up narrative images of Jimmy's roots, and subsequent

---

[46]Swaggart, *To Cross.*

reminders that his heritage was, after all, much like theirs. Historian David Edwin Harrell observed the value in Swaggart's approach: "Swaggart's a very talented guy, and essentially what he's done is to go back to first base and start holding crusades around the country, which is how he started out."[47] By reminding Swaggart's people how he started out, he reminds them how humble his beginnings were.

There was also a very practical dimension to Swaggart's decision to return to the highways and byways. Just as politicians often return to small towns to solidify their grass roots support, so Swaggart chose to go to where the people were. Harrell explains: "It seems his strategy is to take to the circuit and rebuild from the bottom up. Swaggart can take his talents and go back to the grass roots and rebuild. Many of these people (TV evangelists) are nothing more than media personalities. That's not the case with Swaggart."[48] The power of the boy from humble beginnings narrative lies in the promises it holds to those that hear it. Reflecting upon Swaggart's appeal, one author explained: "He is the local boy made good to millions of Americans. By giving their pittance to his ministry, the poor donors in the trailer parks and tract homes along streets nobody ever heard of and in towns that barely make it on the highway map, are realizing their own dreams. They, too, can share in the glory and power of the ministry."[49]

New and Improved Jimmy Swaggart

Perhaps no narrative found its way into the rhetoric of Swaggart more often than the story of adversity leading to better things. Along the way of his rhetorical journey, Swaggart proclaimed:

---

[47]David E. Harrell, as quoted in Gustav Niebuhr, "TV Evangelists Rebound From Viewer Erosion," *Atlanta Journal* 1 May, 1989 (Newsbank SOC file 40: C6).

[48]David E. Harrell, quoted in Greg Garrison, "After the Fall," *Birmingham News* 7 May, 1989 (Newsbank SOC file 40: C9).

[49]Joel Kovel, "Jimmy Swaggart's Crystal Palace," *Zeta Magazine* (April 1988): 78.

By the help and grace of God, Jimmy Swaggart is a better man now. . . . By the help and grace of God, he will be a better preacher.[50]

Jimmy Swaggart is not the same man today as I was six months ago. I believe my message will reflect a deeper compassion and love and an even greater voracity against sin, but delivered with tenderness. Some have said to me, "Brother Swaggart, we could relate to your message; the anointing was on it; however, we were never quite able to relate to you. But now we can relate to you."[51]

I'm going to love the sinner, and I'm going to love the unlovable. I'm going to love the Christian, I'm going to love the Baptist, I'm going to love the Methodist.[52]

The great burden that God has given me to touch this world for Jesus Christ has not lifted. It has rather intensified.[53]

You will see a different Jimmy Swaggart. You will see a man with more compassion, more love, and more understanding.[54]

I want to serve notice on the devil and all the demons of hell: the best is yet to come![55]

Added to these were the following statements made by Frances Swaggart just prior to her husband's comeback sermon:

---

[50] Swaggart, "A Personal Message," 2.
[51] Swaggart, quoted in Dunne, "Swaggart to Oversee," (Newsbank: E7).
[52] Swaggart, as quoted in Dunne, "Evangelist Says," (Newsbank: E12).
[53] Swaggart, "I Just Want," 12.

[54] Swaggart, quoted in Case and Cutbirth, 26.
[55] Swaggart, quoted in Dunne, "Evangelist Says," (Newsbank: E12).

I love him (Jesus Christ) more than I have ever loved him before. . . . I have always had a burden for souls and a love for humanity but I think that has increase today more than ever before because now when I look at people and they are hurting, I can not only sense their hurt. I can feel their hurt. I can actually feel the pain (see Appendix B).

Grounds ------------> Warrants ------------> Minor Claims ----------> Major Claims

Grounds	Warrants	Minor Claims	Major Claims
I have now succumbed to temptation.	"All things work together for good to them that love God, to them that are the called according to his purpose."(Rom. 12:1)	I will be more understanding.	I am worthy of forgiveness and continued support.
I have now experienced great pain and suffering.		I will be more loving.	
I have now experienced fierce criticism.	Once you personally experience something, you are better able to relate to others who share that experience.	I will be more forgiving.	
I have now experienced abandonment by those that claimed to love me.		I will be an even better preacher and minister than I was before.	
		Conclusion: Not only is this ordeal not a negative thing, but it is actually a good thing.	

In his fall, Jimmy Swaggart had become one of them. In that incarnation into the humanity of the common man, Swaggart became capable of bringing his audience to new heights, to a new closeness to their God. Not only was the fall of Swaggart not something to grieve over; it was the vehicle by which Swaggart, and ultimately his audience, would be brought closer to God.

6

THE OUTCOME:
SUCCESS AND ADVERSITY

When the worst, most sin-benighted, hell-bound, fourfold child of
Hell staggers down the aisle and falls at the feet of the world's
redeemer, God looks at Him and announces to the whole heavens: "I
find no fault in him!!!

—The final words of Jimmy Swaggart's Comeback Sermon

SWAGGART MADE ARGUMENTS. MOST OF HIS ARGUMENTS WERE
formed out of the cloth of doctrinal presuppositions and rhetorical
narratives. Weaving all of the strands of those arguments together, a
pattern emerged: Swaggart reasoned that he was not at fault; the blame
should be laid at the feet of Satan, the pornography industry, and other
believers. Moreover, even if he was to shoulder some of the blame, the
reasons for his mistakes were to be applauded. No matter who was to
blame, his audience must never forget that the ministry and the
minister, as a result of this unfortunate event, would be better than
ever.

As we have observed on numerous occasions, the campaign worked
very well. Indeed, until Swaggart's second tryst with a prostitute,
Swaggart was clearly headed back towards the top of the religious
television ratings. That was only possible if his audience were given a
set of reasons on which they could hang their moral hats. Therefore, it
is not accurate to account for his success simply by observing that
Swaggart's audience was primarily composed of little old southern
ladies, as some in the media have chosen to do.[1] For regardless of their

---

[1]Elizabeth Hardwick, "Church Going," *New York Review*, 8 August 1988, 30.

age, gender, or regional affiliation, this audience demanded a rationale that was consistent with their world view in order to justify Swaggart's request for forgiveness and restoration. Swaggart offered such a rationale, and many of his supporters gladly accepted it.

SWAGGART'S SINCERITY

One of the questions invariably asked about a speaker's apology deals with the question of the apologist's sincerity. Was the speaker truly sorry for what he or she had done, or was his or her apology simply a calculated attempt at damage control? To many the sincerity of Swaggart's remorse remains very much in doubt. True remorse would have led him to apologize sometime before Gorman forced his hand. After all, four months passed between the Gorman confrontation and Swaggart's confession. Only when Gorman shared the photographs with the Assemblies of God Presbytery did Swaggart suddenly feel the need to let the world know of his sorrow for his deeds.

The thoroughness of the comeback campaign is also noteworthy. It certainly appeared to have been a carefully crafted, intentional, well thought-out defense of his behavior. There were simply too many specific lines of argument that led directly to his claim of "I am worthy of forgiveness and continued support" to believe that all of this campaign just somehow worked its way out. Swaggart knew what he wanted and he developed a rhetorical plan to achieve his goal.

Of course, the most likely scenario is that Swaggart's response was more complex than the "he was sincere" or "he wasn't sincere" dichotomy allows. Chances are he was a man possessed of both true guilt and remorse *and* an insatiable desire to engage in damage control. The desires to serve and minister to others, and to achieve wealth, fame, and power probably are at war within him, as they are in most people. We may never know for sure, but we can see the recaptured success that his rhetorical campaign brought him.

BROADER ISSUES

This study has demonstrated that many doctrines primarily addressing one's relationship with God can be transformed into supporting a person's relationship with another person. Swaggart used the doctrines of glossolalia, sin, forgiveness, redemption, baptism of the Holy Spirit, and the blessed hope to suggest that his audience should renew their commitment to Swaggart and his ministry. Clearly, it appears that not only do believers want to be close to God, but they want to be close to those who are close to God.

This study reminds us that arguments are not always obvious. Unless the critic is conversant with the shared world views of speaker and audience, the significance and meaning of certain utterances may escape notice. When Swaggart spoke in tongues, he argued. When Swaggart prayed, he argued. And when Swaggart quoted from his truth source, the Bible, he argued. Claims, warrants, and grounds were often unstated, but an examination of the doctrinal premises of both speaker and audiences surely helped us to see the whole picture. Thus, it may not only be difficult to decipher the meaning of arguments, but it may be difficult to even discover the existence of arguments. The critic must dive into the pool of shared community meaning, or that critic may not notice the presence of arguments that lie below the surface.

Edwin Black asserts that one of the differences between the scientist and the critic is the interest in making criticism a "force in society."[2] This study has demonstrated that in order to do that, the critic need not take any particular ethical stance with regard to the rhetor or the artifact. I have made few implicit claims concerning the veracity of Swaggart's arguments, the intent of Swaggart's heart and mind, or the effect of the discourse on the larger society. Yet the critic can take such a stance and still perform a vital social service by simply "translating the

---

[2]Edwin Black, *Rhetorical Criticism: A Study in Method* (Madison: University of Wisconsin Press, 1965), 5.

object of his criticism into the terms of his audience and in part by educating his audience to the terms of the object."[3]

THE REST OF THE STORY: 1988 TO THE PRESENT

From the outset this book has been a story of success. That would be true if the story ended before June 1991. This would prove to be the turning point that would include too many scandalous events for Swaggart's primary audience once again to forgive and forget. But prior to that date, things almost returned to normal for Swaggart. The days immediately following his three month rhetorical campaign to salvage his empire found him in busy preparation for his upcoming preaching tour. The first stop on the tour occurred on July 22, 1988, as Swaggart arrived in Indianapolis for a three day crusade. Organizers publicly expected upwards of eight thousand people to attend, despite the fact that the Assemblies of God leadership expressly forbade their constituents to attend the crusade.[4] Although no exact attendance figures were available, it is quite certain that the crowds turned out to be considerably smaller than anticipated.

Despite the disappointing beginning, prospects were improving for Swaggart by the end of crusades in Indiana, California, and Texas. Swaggart reported that the ministries operated in the black in October for the first time since the scandal, and Swaggart energized his supporters with news of seemingly monumental evangelistic significance: the ministry had signed an agreement to air their program in the People's Republic of China. Chinese officials reportedly asked for $250,000 a month in exchange for an estimated 330 million weekly viewers. What Swaggart failed to tell his audience was that the shows were dramatically edited, and in the Chinese versions Swaggart was not even allowed to speak or preach. In fact, the only appearances Swaggart was allowed to make in the edited versions were as a singer.

---

[3]Ibid., 6.

[4]Carol Elrod, "Swaggart Faithful Traveling Far to See Comeback Revival," *Indianapolis Star*, 22 July 1988 (Newsbank SOC file 76: E14).

In February 1989, Swaggart again found himself charged with sexual improprieties. The February edition of *Penthouse* magazine reported that Catherine Mary Kampen, an exotic dancer from Louisiana, claimed to have had an affair with Swaggart similar to the one described by Debra Murphree in 1988. Swaggart vehemently denied the charge and vowed to sue *Penthouse* for its libelous story.[5] As it turned out, this charge may indeed have been a false one, since the woman's story turned out to be inconsistent. Little became of the charges since very few individuals, including those counted among Swaggart's critics, believed its veracity.

Swaggart enjoyed a relatively quiet 1989 and 1990. But beginning in June 1991, events began to emerge that would spell the beginning of the end for Swaggart. On June 28, 1991, CNN broadcast a report on Swaggart that included the photographs that Gorman had used to confront Swaggart. The pictures showed Swaggart, dressed in a red shirt, white pants, and a head band, walking in and out of a room in the Travel Inn Motel with Debra Murphree. When Swaggart was asked about the report, he replied: "the Holy Spirit (told me) at about 10:00 a.m. on Wednesday not to defend myself against anything."[6] The publication of the photographs was especially troubling to Swaggart, for in the peaceful environment of 1989 and 1990, Swaggart had been moving more and more to a stance of absolute denial concerning the original charge. For example, when asked in 1989 about the details of the scandal, Swaggart responded:

> What actually happened had little resemblance to what was portrayed over television, was reported in the press, and was fantasized by some preachers. Satan took what actually happened and turned and twisted it for one purpose only. That purpose? To destroy our integrity, our character, and the

---

[5]Lyn Cryderman, "Centerfold Follies," *Christianity Today*, 17 March 1989, 17.

[6]Mark Lambert, "CNN Broadcast 'Hurts' Swaggart," *Baton Rouge Morning Advocate*, 29 June 1991 (Newsbank SOC file 67: B7).

confidence that people have in us. And he used pornographers and preachers to do it."[7]

Swaggart's ability to use his followers' short memories was crippled as the nation was invited to see the most damning evidence for themselves.

On July 8, 1991, things turned even worse as the Marvin Gorman defamation of character trial finally began. Gorman charged Swaggart and other key Swaggart ministry officials with intentionally and willfully attempting to destroy Gorman and his ministries by spreading false information about Gorman's moral indiscretions. Gorman had admitted to one affair, but letters sent by Swaggart to denomination officials claimed knowledge of some "one hundred" acts of adultery.[8] On September 12, the ninety million dollar lawsuit was decided in Gorman's favor, with Swaggart ordered to pay Gorman and his debtors ten million dollars. Not surprisingly, Swaggart appealed the decision, which he won later that year. In May 1994, the two sides settled out of court for an undisclosed amount of money.

I encountered Swaggart in person for the first time on the final day of his San Diego crusade on October 6, 1991. My wife Barbara and I arrived 45 minutes early and took a seat ten rows from the stage. There were already approximately a thousand people in their seats, and Swaggart's son Donnie was at the pulpit, touting different promotional items. As we took our seats, Donnie was advertising a "crusade special: if you buy three tapes, we'll give you a fourth one free." He was referring to the items on one of the twenty tables set up just outside the auditorium that were full of everything from Swaggart's books and tapes to jewelry.

By the time the service began, most of the approximately two thousand attendees were seated. The ethnic makeup of the crowd was consistent with the makeup of greater San Diego, with half of the

---

[7]Simoneaux, "One Year Later" (Newsbank: F3).

[8]Joe Gyan Jr., "Swaggart Tells Jury Gorman 'is Still Lying," *Baton Rouge Morning Advocate,* 7 August 1991 (Newsbank SOC file 87: B7).

audience comprised of blacks or Hispanics. Six television cameras were in place as the band began to play a lively rendition of a gospel hymn. Swaggart quietly took a seat towards the back of the platform.

After a number of songs, the chairman of the crusade committee—a local Pentecostal pastor, called Swaggart to the podium to present him with a plaque for his service to Christ. Before the pastor sat down, he twice remarked, "You cynics, you cannot deny the fruit!" Swaggart then spoke for the first time, thanking the committee for the honor. Among his brief comments were, "We have hurt until there is no more blood to bleed. . . . No preacher went through this with us. You have restored this preacher."

After a few more lively songs, Swaggart again approached the pulpit saying, "I'm an evangelist, so I have to take an offering." He then invited anyone who had given or was giving at least fifty dollars to come down to the front to shake his hand and to receive a Jimmy Swaggart Ministries Bible. Approximately fifty individuals stood in line for that privilege.

After the offering, Swaggart took to the pulpit for his sermon. The style was exactly as it was described in chapter two, but experiencing Swaggart's preaching in person gave me a much greater appreciation for Swaggart's rhetorical power. Frankly, I have never seen an audience so enthralled by a public speaker. On his command they would sing, dance and run around the room, and Swaggart made it all seem like the appropriate response.

Swaggart based his sermon on John 7:37, "If any man is thirsty, let him come to Me and drink." But most of his sermon could better be described as a compilation of emotional stories and statements than it could be considered a sermon organized around one developed theme. These are just a few of the comments that brought the crowd to a frenzy:

> If your church has no Jesus in it, you'll have no problem with the world. If your church has a little Jesus in it, you'll have a little problem with the world. If your church has much Jesus in it, you have much problems with the world. And if your church

has all of Jesus in it, you'll catch hell—but you're going to heaven! . . . When churches turn against you and your name is a joke and you pray to die and no man careth for my soul—at the darkest, you hear him whisper (Swaggart pauses and then whispers) I love you. Devil, do you hear that?!! You slimy rascal, perk up your pointy little ears. My Lord said, "I will never leave you!!"

There was a gentleman sitting in the seat next to me. He had all of the appearances of being homeless. At one especially dramatic moment in Swaggart's sermon, the man got out of his seat and ran straight towards Swaggart. Based on his appearance and his actions, four "ushers" quickly took a position to intercept him. This, of course, got the crowd's attention, but Swaggart, without so much as a pause, proclaimed, "those of you that thought he was out of his mind need to be reminded what its like to be Spirit filled!" He and the band then broke into *fifteen* verses of "Breathe on Me Spirit." By the end of the song, the crowd was in an absolute frenzy.

At the conclusion of the sermon, Swaggart gave a public altar call, but instead of inviting people to accept Christ, the invitation was for people to become Spirit filled and speak in tongues. As virtually the entire audience came forward, he commanded them all to begin to speak in tongues. Except for my wife and me, not one person in the audience was not at least attempting to do so. Clearly, this was a doctrinally compatible community.

Little did I know that this would be Swaggart's last crusade for a long, long time. Five days later, on October 11, 1991, Swaggart was pulled over by a policeman in the small town of Indio, California. Inside the car were dozens of pornographic magazines, and one of the town's few prostitutes. The prostitute reported that Swaggart had picked her up, asking if she was "working." When Swaggart noticed the policemen behind him, he panicked, which caused the erratic driving that motivated the policemen to pull Swaggart over.

The press got hold of the story the same day, and by the next afternoon, Swaggart was holding a press conference. He explained that he was canceling his remaining crusades, but that the Holy Spirit had told him not to step down as pastor or televangelist. The next Sunday, he preached in the Family Worship Center as if nothing had happened.

Swaggart has survived since 1991 but he has certainly not thrived. In June 1992 I interviewed Greg Garland of the *Baton Rouge Morning Advocate* concerning Swaggart's status.[9] Garland reported that Swaggart was still preaching, but that the congregation numbers were so low that a sizable portion of the Family Worship Center auditorium had been curtained off. The college, which at one time was running over six thousand students, enrolled less than a hundred. And although he was still broadcasting on a few stations, most of his television contracts had been canceled, and many were in lawsuits over payment. Clearly, it appeared that even a doctrinal community can be challenged to forgive and forget once too often.

Garland reported that the most talked about fact concerning Swaggart was his obsession with an anti-psychiatry/psychology stance. Garland stated that, according to his observations as well as the observations of those who attend the weekly services, Swaggart finds a way to attack the psychiatric profession in virtually every one of his sermons. During one service that Garland attended, Swaggart proclaimed, "when Christ was in the wilderness, psychologists would have said that he was suicidally depressed. Psychologists would say he is having delusions." Garland felt that in light of a number of reports that Swaggart may be suffering from mental instability, he had chosen to fight back with a direct attack.

Finally, Garland believed that Swaggart was going to attempt a secret departure from the Baton Rouge area. Garland reported that Swaggart secretly put his house up for sale, but once the press learned of the story, Swaggart took the house off the market and denied it had ever been for sale in the first place.

The last few years have been especially difficult for the ministry. In 1997, his program was being carried on thirty-nine stations, as opposed to 287 stations in 1988. By 1997, his college enrolled forty students,

---

[9] Greg Garland, telephone interview, 9 June 1992.

while his church attendance averaged less than five hundred attendees. In 1998, former ministry employee Barbara Nauer wrote *Jimmy Swaggart: Dead Man Rising*, in which she blamed many of the ministry's problems on the authoritarian rule of Swaggart's wife Frances, whom she labeled the "Empress of Everything."[10] In addition, Swaggart had to endure yet another scandal accusation, this time at the hands of CNN's "Impact" program.[11] According to reporter John Camp, while Swaggart's ministries were drowning in debt, the Swaggart family itself relaxed in luxury due to real estate dealings made with ministry land holdings. Camp claimed that the Swaggart's made $600,000 annually in 1995, while in 1996, the ministry bought each of them a new Mercedes, together valued at $250,000. Camp also reported a December 1995 incident in which Swaggart was stopped by police while he cruised up and down "the Strip" of Baton Rouge, a locale frequented by prostitutes. When confronted with the allegation, Swaggart claimed that he was out there to inspect one of the ministries' radio broadcast towers, even though it was late at night and, as Camp later revealed, the ministry had sold that particular tower over a year earlier.

With his descent into obscurity, Swaggart joins an ever growing list of religious television personalities who found it difficult to live in the public eye with moral integrity. But in the closing moments of his comeback sermon eleven years earlier, Jimmy Lee Swaggart built to one final climactic vocal epiphany with these words:

> Behold the Lamb of God, which taketh away the sin-singular; all of it. No sin that's unpaid; He said "I am now bearing it all. I have every bit of it. I leave nothing out. The alcoholic can go free. The drug addict can go free. The liar can tell the truth." Praise God, whosoever will may come. It is finished![12]

---

[10]Barbara Nauer, *Jimmy Swaggart: Dead Man Rising* (Baton Rouge: Glory Arts, 1988), 116.

[11]"CNN's Impact," reporter John Camp, CNN, 12 September 1997.

[12]Swaggart in "The Jimmy Swaggart Broadcast," 22 May 1988 (Appendix B: 238).

When Swaggart uttered these words, maybe his decision not to mention sexual promiscuity among the litany of sins that were eradicated by his Redeemer was more than just a strategic omission. Perhaps he also knew that, at least for *this* "sin-benighted, Hell-bound, four-fold child of Hell,"[13] more tragic failures lay ahead. He had told stories and had reminded his people of doctrinal truths—and for the moment, he was forgiven.

Indeed, if one of the hallmarks of truth is its ability to withstand the test of time, then Thomas à Kempis's observation, penned over 500 years ago, stands as a prophetic warning to the fate of televangelists, both past and future: "No man can live in the public eye without risk to his soul."[14]

---

[13]Ibid.

[14]Thomas á Kempis, *The Imitation of Christ* , trans. Leo Sherley-Price (New York: Penguin, 1952), 50.

APPENDICES

APPENDIX A

The following is the text of Jimmy Swaggart's apology sermon, delivered February 21, 1988 at the Family Worship Center in Baton Rouge, Louisiana.

Everything that I will attempt to say to you this morning will be from my heart. I will not speak from a prepared script. Knowing the consequences of what I will say and that much of it will be taken around the world, as it should be, I am positive that all that I want to say I will not be able to articulate as I would desire.

But I would pray that you will somehow feel the anguish, the pain, and the love of my heart. I have always—every single time that I have stood before a congregation and a television camera—I have met and faced the issues head-on. I have never sidestepped or skirted unpleasantries. I have tried to be like a man and to preach this gospel exactly as I have seen it without fear or reservation or compromise. I can do no less this morning.

I do not plan in any way to whitewash my sin. I do not call it a mistake, a mendacity; I call it sin. I would much rather, if possible—and in my estimation it would not be possible—to make it worse than less than it actually is. I have no one but myself to blame. I do not lay the fault or the blame of the charge at anyone else's feet. For no one is to blame but Jimmy Swaggart. I take the responsibility. I take the blame. I take the fault.

Many times I have addressed the media in a very stern manner and I have chastised them for what I thought and believed was error in their reporting or their investigation even. This time I do not. I commend them. I feel that the media, both in print and by television, radio, have been fair and objective and even compassionate.

Ted Koppel on "Nightline," I feel, did everything within his power, in going the second, third, fourth, fifth, tenth mile to make doubly certain that what he reported was at least as fair and as honest as he, the spokesman for this world-famed news program, could make it. And I thank him for his objectivity, his kindness and his fairness.

And I also want to express appreciation to the entire media everywhere, but especially here in Baton Rouge—Channels 9, 2 and 33, the newspapers, the radio stations. They've been hard, but they have been fair. They have been objective and at times, I believe, they have even been compassionate—even my old nemesis, John Camp, that we have disagreed with very strongly. And I love you, John. And in spite of our differences, I think you are one of the finest investigative reporters in the world—and I mean that.

I want to address myself as best as I know how to those that I have wronged, that I have sinned against. First of all, my wife, Frances—God never gave a man a better helpmate and companion to stand beside him. And as far as this gospel has been taken through the airwaves to the great cities of the world and covered this globe, it would never have been done were it not for her strength, her courage, her consecration to her Redeemer, the Lord Jesus Christ. I have sinned against you. And I beg your forgiveness.

God said to David 3,000 years ago, you have done this thing in secret, but I will do what I do openly before all of Israel. My sin was done in secret, and God has said to me, "I will do what I do before the whole world." Blessed be the name of the Lord.

God could never give a man, a father, a minister of the gospel, a finer son than he has given me and his mother—Donnie and my beautiful and lovely daughter-in-law, Debbie. Donnie has stood with me. I have relied upon him. And in these trying days, his mother and myself, we do not know what we would have done without his strength, his courage and his utter devotion to the Lord Jesus Christ. Donnie and Debbie, I have sinned against you and I beg you to forgive me.

To the Assemblies of God, which helped bring the gospel to my little beleaguered town when my family was lost without Jesus—this movement and fellowship that . . . has been more instrumental in taking this gospel through the . . . night of darkness to the far-flung hundreds of millions than maybe in the effort in annals of human history. Its leadership has been compassionate and kind and considerate and long-suffering toward me without exception, but never for one moment condoning sin, both on the national level and this esteemed district level. But to its thousands and thousands of pastors that are godly, that uphold the standard of righteousness, its evangelists that are heralds and criers of redemption, its missionaries on the front lines . . . holding back the path of hell—I have sinned against you and I have brought disgrace and humiliation and embarrassment upon you. I beg your forgiveness.

This church [Family Worship Center], this ministry, this Bible college [Jimmy Swaggart Bible College], these professors, this choir, these musicians, these singers that have stood with me on a thousand crusade platforms around the world, that have labored unstintedly [sic] and tirelessly to lift up that great name of Jesus Christ, to tell the weary that He is rest, and the sin-cursed that He, Jesus, is victory, my associates—and no evangelist ever had a greater group of men and women, given by the hand of God—have stood with me unstintedly [sic], unflaggingly. I have sinned against you. I have brought shame and embarrassment to you. I beg your forgiveness.

To my fellow television ministers and evangelists, you that are already bearing an almost unbearable load, to continue to say and tell the great story of Jesus' love, I have made your load heavier and I have hurt you. Please forgive me for sinning against you.

And to the hundreds of millions that I have stood before in over a hundred countries of the world and I've looked into the cameras and so many of you with a heart of loneliness, needing help, have reached out to the minister of the gospel as a beacon of light. You that are nameless—most I will never be able to see except by faith. I have sinned against you. I beg you to forgive me.

And most of all, to my Lord and my Savior, my Redeemer, the One whom I have served and I love and I worship. I bow at His feet, who has saved me and washed me and cleansed me. I have sinned against You, my Lord. And I would ask that Your precious blood would wash and cleanse every stain, until it is in the seas of God's forgetfulness, never to be remembered against me anymore.

I say unto you that watch me today, through His mercy, His grace and His love, the sin of which I speak is not a present sin; it is a past sin. I know that so many would ask why, why? I have asked myself that 10,000 times through 10,000 tears. Maybe Jimmy Swaggart has tried to live his entire life as though he were not human. And I have thought that with the Lord, knowing He is omnipotent and omniscient, that there was nothing I could not do—and I emphasize with His help and guidance. And I think this is the reason (in my limited knowledge) that I did not find the victory I sought because I did not seek the help of my brothers and my sisters in the Lord. I have had to come to the realization that this gospel is flawless even though it is ministered at times by flawed men. If I had sought the help of those that loved me, with their added strength, I look back now and know that victory would have been mine. They have given me strength along with the compassion of our Savior in these last few days that I have needed for a long, long time.

Many ask, as I close, this: will the ministry continue? Yes, the ministry will continue. Under the guidance, leadership and directives (as best we know how and can) of the Louisiana District of the Assemblies of God, we will continue to take this gospel of Jesus Christ all over the world. I step out of this pulpit at the moment for an indeterminate period of time and we will leave that in the hands of the Lord.

The Bible college of these young men and young ladies whom I have tried to set a standard for and have miserably failed, its most esteemed president, Ray Tresk—I too, beg you, the future pastors, evangelists and missionaries, to forgive me. But this Bible college will continue.

I close this today with the words of another man that lived 3,000 years ago—and I started to say who committed sin that was worse than mine, but I take that back. And if the Holy Spirit will allow me to borrow his words, I will review that which is as real now as when it was penned in Jerusalem:

"Have mercy upon me, O God. According to thy lovingkindness; according unto the multitude of thy tender mercies, blot out my transgressions. Wash me thoroughly from mine iniquity, and cleanse me from my sin. For I acknowledge my transgressions; and my sin is ever before me.

"Against thee, thee only, have I sinned and done this evil in thy sight, that thou mightest be justified when thou speakest, and be clear when thou judgest. Behold, I was shapen in iniquity; and in sin did my mother conceive me. Behold, thou desirest truth in the inward parts; and in the hidden parts thou shalt make me to know wisdom.

"Purge me with hyssop, and I shall be clean; wash me, and I shall be whiter than snow. Make me to hear joy and gladness; that the bones which thou hast broken may rejoice. Hide thy face from my sins,and blot out all mine iniquities.

"Create in me a clean heart, O God; and renew a right spirit within me. Cast me not away from thy presence; and take not thy holy spirit from me. Restore unto me the joy of thy salvation; and uphold me with thy free spirit. Then will I teach transgressors thy ways; and sinners shall be converted unto thee. Deliver me from bloodguiltiness, O God, thou God of my salvation: and my tongue shall sing aloud of thy righteousness. O Lord, open thou my lips; and my mouth shall shew forth thy praise.

"For thou desirest not sacrifice; else would I give it; thou delightest not in a broken spirit; a broken and a contrite heart, O God, thou wilt not despise. Do good in thy good pleasure unto Zion; build thou the walls of Jerusalem. Then shalt thou be pleased with the sacrifices of righteousness, with burnt offering and with whole burnt offering; then shall they offer bullocks upon thine altar." [Ps. 51]

Thank you. Thank you and God bless you.

APPENDIX B

The following is the text of the television broadcast of the comeback sermon preached by Jimmy Swaggart on May 22, 1988 at the Family Worship Center in Baton Rouge.

JIMMY SWAGGART

It is so good to see you today. And I don't have to tell you how happy I am to be here. Not me but Jesus, Jesus, Jesus, Jesus, Jesus, Jesus, Jesus, Jesus. Praise God; praise the Lord. We are here strictly, totally, absolutely, completely on his mercy, his love, his grace; and we thank him for that. Totally and completely we praise God. I want to thank you—so many of you for coming distances: so many of you have. And this means so much to this evangelist, our family; your love that you have shown in the midst of a most trying time. Those of you that are right here we are so glad you are here. So many of you have been so gracious, so considerate to us as well. I don't think any of you have been mean to us. All of you have been so good, so gracious to us. And we love you so very very much. I could say an awful lot and I want to about so many of the people who have helped us and stood with us and the pastors of this church and the ministers in the ministry itself. But I would invariably leave out someone if I were to do that and that would be someone I would not want to leave out; so I will let discretion be the better part of valor on that. But I will ask Frances and Donnie and Debbie to step out here. And you can't know the load and the burden that these have had to bear the past months and I have leaned on them second only to the Lord. And to say that I love them would be the classic understatement of all of my life. They mean more to me than words could ever begin to say. And I want to thank you for taking the responsibility that you have done.

Donnie Swaggart

When the Lord calls a person to a position of responsibility the responsibility doesn't change when there is difficulty or distress. It has been an honor to assume responsibility.

Jimmy Swaggart

The one I have leaned on through that: this is the greatest wife that God ever gave any preacher. I love you.

Frances Swaggart

I thank the Lord for His grace and His love and His mercy. You know we have lived for the Lord Jesus many, many years but yet never has He been as real and as close as He has been these past few months. He has been our strength. He has been our source, our sustenance. He has been our everything and not once has He failed us. And there have been many dark nights and there have been many dark days but there have always been the bright times. And when those bright times came, through them, Jesus Christ. I love Him today with all my heart and I love Him more than I have ever loved Him before and you know I have always felt that. I have always had a burden for souls and a love for humanity but I think that has increased today more than ever before because now, when I look at people and their hurting, I can not only sense their hurt; I can feel their hurt. I can actually feel the pain. And when you are a laborer in the Lord Jesus Christ's work, I think that it is so important that when you look at people, you know people. God loves you. You are what He gave his life for. He died for humanity and He loves us more than we can ever, ever know; and when you can sense the pain and the suffering in another individual, then you are closer to Jesus Christ, I think, than you might realize. Our heart, our burden, and our souls are for the work of the Lord Jesus Christ. To be able to stand before you and tell you about Jesus and minister to you means more than, it's our heart and I thank God for that privilege that He has given to us. We love you. God bless you.

JIMMY SWAGGART

This little song this morning, I think probably most, if not all, of you would know it. But it is those that are timeless that are written by the inspiration, I think, of the Holy Ghost.

SONG

His blood washes white as snow. Oh the blood of Jesus. Oh the blood of Jesus. Oh the blood of Jesus. It washes white as snow. Oh the blood of Jesus. Oh the blood of Jesus. Oh the blood of Jesus. It washes white as snow.

Our God reigns. Our God reigns. Our God reigns. Our God reigns. He's alive. He's alive. He's alive. He's alive. Our God reigns. One day he is going to come back. Our God reigns. Crowned King of Kings and Lord of Lords. Our God reigns. And the whole world will bow at his feet and say our God reigns. Our God reigns. Our God reigns. Our God reigns. Our God reigns.

One more time.

Our God reigns. Our God reigns. Our God reigns. Our God reigns.

We'll talk it over in the bye and bye. We'll talk it over my sweet Lord and I. I'll ask the reason; he'll tell my why. When we talk it over when we talk it over in the bye and bye.

One more time (repeat)

I'll never be lonely again. Never again. For I have opened my heart and should to him. I'll brush away the tears. Forget my foolish fears. Never be lonely again. Never again.

Just one more time (repeat)

SERMON: THE PRIZE OF THE HIGH CALLING (JIMMY SWAGGART)

If you have your Bibles, will you turn with me please to the Book of Philippians Chapter 3, one of the prison epistles while Paul was incarcerated in Rome. I have preached, stood, before some of the largest crowds in the world but I guess I stand now with more fear and trembling than I have ever before in my whole life.

Paul said, starting with the 7th verse:

"But what things were gained to me, those I count as lost for Christ. Yea doubtless, and I count all things as lost for the excellency of the knowledge of Christ Jesus my Lord: for whom I have suffered the loss of all things, and do count them as done that I may win Christ. And be found in him, not having my own righteousness, that is of the law but that which is through the faith of Christ. The righteousness which is of God by faith that I may know him and the power of his resurrection and the fellowship of his sufferings being made conformable unto his death. If by any means I might attain unto the resurrection of the dead, not as though I had already attained, either were already perfect, but I follow after, if that that I may apprehend him, that for which also I am apprehended. But this one thing I do, forgetting those things which are behind and reaching forth unto those things which are before. I press toward the mark for the prize of the high calling of God in Christ Jesus."

I would pray that God would help me the rest of my life wherever He would choose to take me and this ministry. It is His, I am His. If He sees fit for me to sweep floors in a mission (and I mean this, I am not being self-serving; I mean it in my heart), in a little mission across the track, I would be honored to anything for Him and do it the rest of my life. But whatever He may choose for me to do I want to somehow, in greater measure that I have ever been able to do so before, to show His love and His grace and mercy and His compassion and His long-suffering to a heartbroken world. I want to use for a subject the prize of the high calling.

Requests for Contributions

Donnie, I want you to put on the screen and kinda let it flash on and off or whatever you do, "SAVE YOUR STATION." And I want to talk to you from the very bottom of my heart for just a few moments.

Someone said to me the other day, "Brother Swaggart, it always seems you are in need of funds" and, of course, that's the truth because we are constantly trying to carry out the great commission of Jesus Christ to take this gospel to the whole world. That's our business and that's my calling. As I have told you many times in the past few weeks we, of course—naturally—it would be obvious that we—have suffered a terrible blow. And to be frank and plain and honest with you I would not blame you, I do not blame you, for not sending us one dime or one dollar. And I want that to sink in because I mean it from my heart. I don't blame you for not sending anything. But I'm praying that somehow we can get past the human emotions and all the problems that I have, just as you have, and say, "Well, Lord, I love You. And I want this gospel under the anointing of the Holy Spirit, even though it is preached by a crippled preacher, to come into my home, my heart, my life, my community, my city, this nation, the world."

Every day we struggle and we've lost a few stations because we simply did not have enough money to pay the bill. I do not want to lose yours. Every time Shirley comes in and says Brother Swaggart, we were cancelled on thus and so; it is just like someone taking a dagger, putting it into my heart and turning it. Because you see, I know. I know two things. I know that people will be lost because of that and I know that Jimmy Swaggart is to blame. Only He could take away that kind of hurt and He will because He is the Healer. I feel that what is done in these days matters more that what I fell or you feel. I believe that many many souls are hanging in the balance and that is what hurts so much because I know what Jesus can do in a heart and a life. I know what He can do. I know how He can change a life. I know He is the only one really that can. And so I guess I am saying: If you can dig down and help me, you will be in effect helping them. Thank you.

ANNOUNCER

To reach out to a lost and dying world with the good news of the gospel of Jesus Christ and to tell of His mercy that redeems us from hell, we need your prayerful and financial support to help prevent this telecast from going off you television station. We are fighting to save ever TV station contract we have for the thousands who have not yet heard the unchanging gospel of Jesus Christ. A station being cancelled means less people will have the opportunity to hear this life-changing message. We must not let this happen. Your diligence in prayer and financial support can help save your station. Please do not hesitate. Write today so that we can continue bring this victorious gospel message into your home.

As a Christian we are to press towards the mark as we run with patience the race set before us. Today evangelist Jimmy Swaggart reveals the prize of the high calling.

JIMMY SWAGGART

A year and a half ago I had two dreams. And, if I remember correctly, they were both in the same night or at least the same week—and I think they were both the same night. I did not understand them. I understand them now—at least in part. I did not understand them then. I related them to Frances and to my staff; some of them wondering at the meaning. As I said, I think I have seen some of it come to pass and I do understand at least a part of it.

I dreamed I was in a church. The church was empty, it was not this one, and I was tied or held down to the floor flat on my back against the far wall. I remember wanting to get to the platform—to the pulpit, but I could not. In that particular church (and I have no idea what church it was, as I have mentioned), in the aisle where I was spread-eagled on my back on the floor unable to get up, the aisle ran vertical. And in that aisle was the largest serpent that I had ever seen up to then. It must of stretched a hundred feet long. It must have been four, five, six feet tall and it stretched the entire length of the church from me to the platform and the pulpit. I did not at that time know what it meant, but I know now what it meant.

And that same night, if it was the same night, I had a similar dream. I, with a sword or a club—I do not remember which, was in a house and I was fighting a serpent. It was large and it attacked me standing as tall as I was and I was fighting the serpent. And I remember the struggle was so intense. There was a man whom I did not know and still do not know, standing in the shadows. He was not evil because of the look on his face that I could see. He was watching me. He stood and looked without comment as I fought this thing; fighting with all the strength I had and finally subdued it and killed it.

I remember how, exhausted, I walked out of the house. He was by my side and once again he seemed to be ethereal, not quite, or surreal; not quite tangible, but he stood there. I was standing exhausted with this club in my hand standing outside of the house and I looked to my right. I thought at first it was a huge concrete pillar standing a hundred or so feet high but then it moved and when it moved it felt like the earth was shaking. And I looked at it and I saw it was another serpent much larger than the one I mentioned a moment ago. It seemed to stand, as I said, a hundred feet or more high; its head darting, its body as large almost as this octagon. And when I looked at it and the man was standing about six feet from me looking at me and looking at this serpent. And I looked at this little club I had in my hand that I had just defeated the one inside with. And the thing moved again and the ground shook. And I remember my knees buckling and I awakened from the dream looking up at it saying "God, I have to fight this and I don't know how to do it." And the dream ended.

I did not know what it meant, but today I know what it meant. And God showed me the ending of the dream. I could not fight that leviathan. I did not fight him. I could not whip him. I could not overcome him within myself. But Jesus Christ overcame him for me.

At 4:15 a.m. one morning just a few weeks ago, I was sobbing and I won't tell you the reason and the things that I ask of my heavenly Father; but I was sobbing and broken. Not one time but this had been many, many times and I happened to look at the watch. I had come down from upstairs and I had laid it on the couch and I was sobbing and literally doubled up weeping and asking my Lord question after question. And I relate to you and I'm showing you the ending of this dream. But I will tell you this. He said to me, spoke to my heart, and said, "Your struggles could never have defeated this enemy. But all I had to do was say, Satan I rebuke thee and he is defeated." Just a simple word when that great Paul wrote the book of Philippians, he made some statements that I would hope to be able to bring to you this morning. And have three little points to this most simplistic of messages: the past, the present, and the future.

When we pertain to the past he said, first of all in the 13th verse, "Brethren, I count not myself to have apprehended" and then he said, "but this one thing I do" the scripture related to us singleness of heart. Paul writes to us, or is it Luke? Paul does, I think, and then the Master related singleness of eye. This one thing I do. I don't know in reading this of Paul's struggles. I have no idea. Paul to me is a giant of giants. I do not know when he wrote this, if he wrote it from his own experience, or he wrote it guided by the Holy Spirit. Either way, of course, for all of mankind that would name the name of Jesus. I have no idea. But he said, "But this one thing I do." It is emphatic. It is a singleness of heart, a singleness of eye. I will not be deterred. This one thing I do, he said, "forgetting those things which are behind." Now I want this thing to sink in a little bit. Forgetting those things which are behind. And the Greek says completely forgetting those things which are behind; completely forgetting them.

Paul will often use athletics, the metaphor of athletic contests, I don't know whether he liked sports or whether the Roman world was sports crazy and he used it, or the Holy Spirit did it to get related to people. I have no idea. But in the Greek it means that as we are in this race we have our eyes on the goal. Those that are behind us, the thudding of their feet that are trying to catch us and overtake us and subdue us and overtake us are right behind us. But Paul is saying I will not even listen to the thudding of their feet, will pay absolutely no attention to the sounds. I will keep my eyes ahead and not look back at those who are running behind me. Doubt. Fear. Unbelief. Past failure. Past sins. Past heartache. I will completely forget them as if they are no longer. They are not there. And I have labored over this and that I bring to you.

I in part realize that if I am to attain and see the present and the future it will be incumbent to me to adhere to this which the Holy Spirit has directed. Completely forget that which is behind. But I am in a terrible position. I am sure there will be many, the media for one, and I do not sit critically, who will see that I do not forget. I realize that it will be the hardest task because this thing has come close to killing Frances, Donnie, and me. You will never know, you will never know the pain. The hurt. Words could never describe it and I am saying God, how can I forget? How is it possible to forget? I know within myself it is impossible but I know one other thing. Jesus Christ is not only a savior, He is a healer. He talked about healing the brokenhearted. A healing is a sore, a gaping wound and then it closes. It doesn't close automatically. It doesn't close instantly. It closes slowly. But when it is finally healed, there is no soreness, no pain left whatsoever. And, if it is a broken bone, when it heals it is stronger even than any other part of the body.

Completely forgetting that which is past. Now how, how, how can this be done? How is it possible to do it? You see and I preach this not only for me but I preach it for you on the television. I preach it for you here in this audience today because guilt is one of Satan's greatest weapons. It is so severe that vocabulary cannot describe it. Guilt that eats away at the vitals. But you must remember this: repentance is not repining. Did you hear me? Repentance does not pan. Guilt pans and guilt is like a cancer. You can't escape it. It's there with you in the lonely hours of the night. It's there when the world is asleep and you remember. And it cuts. And it burns. And it sears. And you can't escape it and you cannot get away from it. Millions of men and women today are holding a bottle of alcohol or a shot glass of liquor because of guilt. Millions today take drugs because of guilt. Psychiatry doesn't have an answer for it. Psychology doesn't have an answer for it. Therapy doesn't have an answer for it.

I want to take you back to the Old Testament to the Book of Leviticus, I think it is the fifth chapter. You don't have to turn to it; it is there. It gives us a detail of the sin offering. This is the old Jewish lexicon, the old Jewish economy. You are here today washed in the blood, saved because of it. And what I am going to give you relates to the poorest of the poor, the poorest of the poor. They could not afford a bullock. They could not afford a lamb. They could not even afford two turtle doves or pigeons. They would come with, and the Scripture gave the exact measurement of, flour; it was enough to make one loaf of bread. And all of it had a vast eternal consequence and significance to it. Jesus didn't die on Calvary two times, three times, or five times. He died once and that was enough. One loaf. God the Holy Ghost told the priest one loaf. They didn't really need the loaf but enough flour for one loaf. And he would come up and give it to the priest and the priest would take that handful of flour which was a type of the life of Christ—the coming Redeemer, the coming Savior, the coming Messiah—and he would go to a brazen altar that burned enflame. Whose embers had been ignited by fires from heaven when Bazeleo had made it and the four horns pointed to the north, the south, the east, and the west and the flames were to never go out. The fire type of God's judgment upon his son, upon me, or upon Jesus. Upon you or upon the Christ. We die or He dies. And the priest would take the flour drop it in the flames without frankincense or oil—specific without frankincense or oil. Frankincense was a type of answered prayer.

And when the Holy Spirit said they cannot put frankincense in it, it was saying when He will hang upon that cross and He will pray for help, and He will say the dogs tear of me. He was speaking of demon spirits and the bulls of Bashan gore me and He would look at that spotless sinless flesh as recorded in Psalm 22, I think it is, and He would say I am but a worm. And He would say my God deliver me. But God would not answer that prayer. No Frankincense because the prayer for the only time in thirty-three and a half years of the life of the Master—the prayer would not be answered. Why? Because there was no oil there either. The oil is a type of a spirit and when He said, "My God, my God, why has Thou forsaken me?" on that cross, the Holy Ghost that had guided His every footstep, directed His every word, moved with Him through time and eternity, hovered over Mary when she conceived of the Spirit and was there with Him as He came up and with Him in the Temple when He was twelve years of age and with Him when He walked off to Jordan, with Him when He raised the dead and opened blinded eyes. There when He said, "Lazarus come forth"—the world has never seen such power. And you talk about Jesus Christ. You are not talking about a sissy. You are talking about God Emmanuel manifested in the flesh who faced Hell's worst, who faced every demon and devil, who faced homosexuality, who faced lesbianism, who faced alcoholism, who faced drug addiction, who faced lying and cheating and thieving and stared Hell right square in the face and overcame (speak in tongues).

I am not on this platform this morning because of anything I have done. Not because of a prayer I prayed, not because of an hour I have confessed, not because of the supplication I have made. I am here because He said, "My God, my God, why hast Thou forsaken me?" and God The Holy Ghost He has never left me. He has never left me. He has never left me. He has never left you and He won't leave you because Jesus paid the price that He will live with you. He said I will never leave you. I will never forsake you. Hell may come your way but I will never leave you or forsake you. Glory to God! Praise the Lord!

The Lord of Glory God Almighty pulled the blinds and said I can't look. A thrice holy God cannot look at sin even if it is borne by His

Son. Jesus said, "It is finished", and when He said "It is finished," He was saying many things. He was saying you no longer have to bring a handful of flour. You no longer have to bring a lamb. Father, I have finished the old economy and paid the price: every sin, every bondage, every darkness. I am bearing it now and I want you to understand not some of the sins but John said, "Behold the Lamb of God, which taketh away the sin"—singular; all of it. No sin that's unpaid He said I am now bearing. I have every bit of it. I leave nothing out. The alcoholic can go free. The drug addict can go free. The liar can tell the truth. Whosoever will may come. It is finished. I have borne it all. I have carried it all. Put the fire out in the brazen altar; it is no longer needed. I have suffered the fire of eternal God. I have borne the judgment and then, when the worst most sin-benighted hell-bound fourfold child of Hell staggers down the aisle and falls at the feet of the world's Redeemer, God looks at him and announces to the whole heaven, "I find no fault in him." Glory to God!

WORKS CITED

Alexander, Danny Lee. "A Rhetorical Analysis of Selected Television Sermons." Ph.D. diss., Texas Women's University, 1983.

Andrews, James R. *The Practice of Rhetorical Criticism*. New York: Longman, 1990.

Arnold, Christa L. and Dean Fadely. *New Directions in Conflict Research and Theory: Conflict-Management Through The Rhetoric of Compliance-Gaining Apologia*. ERIC, 1989. ED 305 607.

_____. *Sex, Sin, and Swaggart: Conflict-Management Through the Rhetoric of Compliance-Gaining Apologia*. ERIC, 1989. ED 313 737.

_____. "Sin is the Cancer on the Body of Christ: Jimmy Swaggart." American Culture Association in the South. Norfolk, 3 October 1991.

Assemblies of God. *Who We Are and What We Believe*. Springfield: Gospel, 1982.

Baehr, Ted. "Was God a Nepotist? Protecting the Electronic Church from Wickedness." *The Evangelist*, March 1988, 35-36.

Bahr, Robert. *Least of All Saints: The Story of Aimee Semple McPherson*. Englewood Cliffs: Prentice, 1979.

Belanger, Gregory. "Swaggart Angers Church Execs While Defending TV Empire." *New Orleans Times-Picayune*, 3 April 1988. Newsbank SOC file 42: F1-2.

Bitzer, Lloyd. "The Rhetorical Situation." *Philosophy and Rhetoric* 1 (January 1968): 1-14.

Black, Edwin. *Rhetorical Criticism: A Study in Method*. Madison: University of Wisconsin Press, 1965.

Bormann, Ernest G. "Symbolic Convergence Theory: A Communication Formulation." *Journal of Communication* 35 (1985): 128-138.

Boule, David. "Swaggart Returns, Says 'Past is Past.'" *Atlanta Journal* 23 May 1988. Newsbank SOC file 61: F8.

Brockreide, Wayne. "Where is Argument?" *Perspectives on Argumentation*. Eds. Robert Trapp and Janice Schuetz. Prospect Heights: Waveland, 1990.

Browne, Ray B. "The Rape of the Vulnerable." *The God Pumpers*. Eds. Marshall Fishwick and Ray B. Browne. Bowling Green: Bowling Green State University Popular Press, 1987.

Burke, Kenneth. *Counter-Statement*. Berkeley: University of California Press, 1931.

————. *A Rhetoric of Motives*. Berkeley: University of California Press, 1969.

Campbell, Karlyn Kohrs and Kathleen Hall Jamieson. Introduction. *Form and Genre Shaping Rhetorical Action*. Eds. Karlyn Kohrs Campbell and Kathleen Hall Jamieson. Falls Church: SCA, 1978.

Cardwell, J.D. *Mass Media Christianity*. Lanham: University Press of America, 1984.

Case, Jacqueline and Craig W. Cutbirth. "The Crucifixion of Jimmy Swaggart: A Religious Apologia." Division of Rhetoric and Public Address. SCA Convention. Chicago, 1 November 1990.

Castaneda, Carol J. "Swaggart: God told Me to Keep Ministry." *USA Today*, 18 October 1991, 3A.

Chapple, Steve. "Whole Lotta Savin' Goin' On." *Mother Jones*, July-August 1986, 37-45.

Conway, Flo and Jim Siegelman. *Holy Terror*. Garden City: Doubleday, 1982.

Corder, Lloyd E. *Charisma and Christianity: Is Jimmy Lee Swaggart A Cynic?* ERIC, 1988. ED 291 119.

Cox, Ervin Samuel. "An Assessment of Jimmy Swaggart's Responses to ABC's WBRZ Documentary From the Perspective of the 'Rhetorical Situation.'" Diss. University of Arizona, 1988.

"Crisis in Baton Rouge." Narrated by Ted Koppel. *Nightline*. ABC News, 23 February 1988.

Cryderman, Lyn. "Centerfold Follies." *Christianity Today*, 17 March 1989, 17.

Davis, David E. *A Structural Analysis of Four Religious Programs: The Effect of Program Structure of Ethos*. ERIC, 1984. ED 249 568.

Duin, Julia. "Battered Swaggart Crusades in Houston." *Houston Chronicle*, 1 October 1988. Newsbank NIN file 282: D8-9.

Dunne, Mike, Curt Eysink, and Doug Leblanc. "Swaggart Subject of Church Probe." *Baton Rouge Morning Advocate*, 20 February 1988. Newsbank SOC file 15: D1-2.

Dunne, Mike. "Evangelist Says He Will Put Past Behind Him." *Baton Rouge Morning Advocate*, 23 May 1988. Newsbank SOC file 53: E12-13.

_____. Telephone interview. 9 July 1990.

_____. "Swaggart to Oversee Troubled Empire Upon Return to Pulpit." *Baton Rouge Morning Advocate*, 22 May 1988. Newsbank SOC file 53: E7-8.

_____. "Swaggart Plea Letters Sent Quickly." *Baton Rouge Morning Advocate*, 18 March 1988. Newsbank SOC file 28: E10-11.

Dupree, James Vincent. "A Burkean Analysis of the Messages of Three Television Preachers: Jerry Falwell, Robert Schuller, and Jimmy Swaggert [sic]." Ph.D. diss. Pennsylvania State University, 1983.

Elrod, Carol. "Swaggart Faithful Traveling Far to See Comeback Revival." *Indianapolis Star*, 22 July 1988. Newsbank SOC file 76: E14.

Farrell, Thomas B. "Narrative in Natural Discourse: On Conversation and Rhetoric." *Journal of Communication* 35 (1985): 109-127.

Finch, Susan. "Jurors: Swaggart Defamed Gorman." *New Orleans Times-Picayune*, 13 September 1991. Newsbank SOC file 87: B5-6.

Fisher, Walter R. "Clarifying the Narrative Paradigm." *Communication Monographs* 56 (1989): 55-58.

_____. *Human Communication As Narration: Toward a Philosophy of Reason, Value, and Action*. Columbia: University of South Carolina Press, 1987.

Fontaine, Charles R. and Lynda K. Fontaine. *Jimmy Swaggart: To Obey God Rather Than Men*. Crockett: Kerusso, 1989.

Foss, Sonja K., Karen A. Foss, and Robert Trapp. *Contemporary Perspectives on Rhetoric*. Prospect Heights: Waveland, 1991.

Fram, Randy. "Did Oral Roberts Go Too Far?" *Christianity Today* 20 January 1987: 43.

Garland, Greg. Telephone interview. 9 June 1992.

Garrison, Greg. "After the Fall." *Birmingham News*, 7 May 1989. Newsbank SOC file 40: C9-11.

Garvey, John. "Truth Flashes: What's Right About Jimmy Swaggart." *Commonweal*, 26 December 1986: 677-678.

Griffin, Charles J. G. "The Rhetoric of Form in Conversion Narratives." *Quarterly Journal of Speech* 76 (1990): 152-163.

Grissett-Welch, Sheila. "Swaggart." *New Orleans Times-Picayune* 2 May 1988. Newsbank SOC file 53: E14+.

Gromacki, Robert G. *The Modern Tongues Movement*. Nutley: Presbyterian and Reformed, 1977.

Grove, Lloyd. "Jimmy Swaggart's Controversial Crusade." *Washington Post* 8 April 1987: A1+.

Gyan, Joe Jr. "Swaggart Tells Jury Gorman 'Is Still Lying.' " *Baton Rouge Morning Advocate*, 7 August 1991. Newsbank SOC file 87: B7-8.

Hadden, Jeffrey K. and Anson Shupe. *Televangelism Power and Politics on God's Frontier*. New York: Holt, 1988.

Hadden, Jeffrey K. and Charles E. Swann. *Prime Time Preachers*. Reading: Addison-Wesley, 1981.

Hardwick, Elizabeth. "Church Going." *New York Review*, 18 August 1988: 15-21.

Hart, Roderick P. *Modern Rhetorical Criticism*. Glenview: Scott, 1990.

_____. "Public Address: Should it be Disinterred?" Public Address Div. Speech Communication Convention. Denver, 10 November 1985.

_____. "The Rhetoric of the True Believer." *Speech Monographs* 4 (1971): 249-61.

Harvey, David A. "TV Preacher Jimmy Swaggart: Why does He Say Those Awful Things About Catholics?" *The God Pumpers*. Ed. Marshall Fishwick and Ray B. Browne. Bowling Green: Bowling Green University Popular Press, 1987.

Hoover, Stewart M. *Mass Media Religion*. Newbury Park: Sage, 1988.

Horton, Michael. Preface. *The Agony of Deceit*. Chicago: Moody, 1990.

Hughes, Loraye and Dean Fadely. "I Have Sinned Against You: A Criticism of Jimmy Swaggart's Apology to the Assemblies of God Ministry." SCA Convention. Atlanta, 31 October 1991.

Hull, Jon D. "The Rise and Fall of 'Holy Joe.'" *Time*, 3 August 1987, 54-55.

Jackson, Robert L. "Rich Life Style Reflects Swaggart Empire's Wealth." *Los Angeles Times*, 14 March 1988. Newsbank SOC file 28: B3-4.

Jamieson, Kathleen Hall. *Eloquence in an Electronic Age*. New York: Oxford University Press, 1988.

"The Jimmy Swaggart Broadcast." Trinity Broadcasting Network. 21 February 1988.

"The Jimmy Swaggart Broadcast." Trinity Broadcasting Network. 22 May 1988.

Kalette, Denise. "Swaggart's 'Repentance' Key to Revival." *USA Today*, 23 February 1988, 1A.

Kaufman, Joanne. "The Fall of Jimmy Swaggart." *People*, 7 March 1988, 35-39.

King, Peter H. "A Defiant Swaggart Returns to the Pulpit." *Los Angeles Times*, 23 May 1988. Newsbank SOC file 53: E10-11.

"The Koppel Report: Televangelism." ABC News, 26 February 1988.

Kovel, Joel. "Jimmy Swaggart's Crystal Palace." *Zeta Magazine*, April 1988: 76-80.

LaFranchi, Howard. "Swaggart Scandal Casts Another Dark Shadow On TV Ministries." *Christian Science Monitor*, 26 February 1988: 3.

Lamb, Robert Paul. *To Cross A River*. Baton Rouge: Swaggart Ministries, 1984.

Lambert, Mark. "CNN Broadcast 'Hurts' Swaggart." *Baton Rouge Morning Advocate*, 29 June 1991. Newsbank SOC file 67: B7-8.

Lippy, Charles H. *Twentieth-Century Shapers of American Popular Religion*. New York: Greenwood, 1989.

"The Living Legacy of Jim Bakker." *U.S. News and World Report*, 6 November 1989, 14.

Lucaites, John Louis and Celeste Michelle Condit. "Re-Constructing Narrative Theory: A Functional Perspective." *Journal of Communication* 35 (1985): 90-108.

MacIntyre, Alasdair. *After Virtue*. Notre Dame: University of Notre Dame Press, 1984.

Matthews, Jay. "Swaggart Undamaged by Bakker Scandal." *Washington Post*, 29 March 1987, A4.

Milam, Cathy. "Aides Say Oral Cast Out Demons From Swaggart." *Tulsa World,* 1 April 1988. Newsbank SOC file 42: E13-14.

McGee, Michael Calvin and John S. Nelson. "Narrative Reason in Public Argument." *Journal of Communication* 35 (1985): 139-155.

"More Troubles on the Broadcast Front." *Christianity Today*, 18 March 1988, 46-47.

Nauer, Barbara. *Jimmy Swaggart: Dead Man Rising*. Baton Rouge: Glory Arts, 1998.

Niebuhr, Gustav. "Scandals' Ripples Rock TV Preachers." *Atlanta Journal,* 5 February 1989. Newsbank SOC file 15: F1.

_____. "TV Evangelists Rebound From Viewer Erosion." *Atlanta Journal*, 1 May 1989. Newsbank SOC file 40: C6-7.

Ostling, Richard N. "The Day of Reckoning Delayed." *Time*, 11 September 1989, 76-77.

_____. "Now It's Jimmy's Turn." *Time*, 7 March 1988, 46-48.

_____. "Power, Glory--and Politics." *Time*, 17 February 1986, 62-69.

_____. "TV's Unholy Row." *Time*, 6 April 1987, 60-67.

_____. "Worshippers on a Holy Roll." *Time*, 11 April 1988, 55.

_____. "Your Money or His Life." *Time*, 26 January 1987, 63.

Percy, Walker. "Science, Language, Literature." *Signposts in a Strange Land*. Ed. Patrick Sanway. New York: Farrar, 1992.

Perelman, Chaim. "Rhetoric and Philosophy." Trans. Henry W. Johnstone, Jr. *Philosophy and Rhetoric*. (January 1968): 15-24.

Poloma, Margaret M. *The Assemblies of God at the Crossroads*. Knoxville: University of Tennessee Press, 1989.

Postman, Neil. *Amusing Ourselves to Death*. New York: Penguin, 1985.

Pratkanis, Anthony and Elliot Aronson. *Age of Propaganda*. New York: Freeman, 1991.

"Preachers' Rejuvenation, April 7-10, 1988." *The Evangelist*, March 1988, 35.

"The Priceless Corner." *The Evangelist*, May/June 1991, 5.

The PTL Club. WCFC, Channel 38, Chicago, 12 December 1987.

The PTL Club. WCFC, Channel 38, Chicago, 12 December 1987.

Pullam, Stephen Jackson. "The Mass Appeal of Jimmy Swaggart: Pentecostal Media Star." SCA Convention. New Orleans, 3-6 November 1988.

_____. "A Rhetorical Profile of Pentecostal Televangelists: Account for the Mass Appeal of Oral Roberts, Jimmy Swaggart, Kenneth Copeland, and Ernest Angley." Ph.D. diss., Indiana University, 1988.

Rein, Irving, Philip Kotler, and Martin Stoller. *High Visibility*. New York: Dodd, 1987.

Rosellini, Lynn. "Of Rolexes and Repentance." *U.S. News and World Report*, 7 March 1988, 62-63.

Rowland, Robert C. "On Limiting the Narrative Paradigm: Three Case Studies." *Communication Monographs* 56 (March 1989): 39-54.

_____. "Narrative: Mode of Discourse of Paradigm?" *Communication Monographs* 54 (1987): 264-275.

_____. "The Value of the Rational World and Narrative Paradigms." *Central States Speech Journal* 39 (Fall/Winter 1988): 204-217.

Rybacki, Daryn and Donald Rybacki. *Communication Criticism*. Belmont: Wadsworth, 1991.

Saperstein, Saundra. "Spreading A $600,000-a-Day Message." *Washington Post*, 7 June 1987, A20.

Schenck-Hamlin, William J., Richard L. Wiseman, and G.N. Georga-carakos. "A Model of Properties of Compliance-Gaining Strategies." *Communication Quarterly* 30 (1982): 92-100.

Schultze, Quentin. Telephone interview, 22 February 1990.

_____. *Televangelism and American Culture*. Grand Rapids: Baker, 1991.

Sharn, Lori and Mike McQueen. "Second Big Scandal Rocks Church." *USA Today*, 22 February 1988, A1.

Simoneaux, Angela. "End of Year Kinder to Swaggart." *Baton Rouge Morning Advocate*, 27 November 1988. Newsbank NIN file 7: F2.

_____. "One Year Later, Swaggart Still Alive and Preaching." *Baton Rouge Morning Advocate*, 19 February 1989. Newsbank SOC file 22: F1-2.

_____. "Swaggart Tells Crowd He's Healed," *Baton Rouge Morning Advocate,* 26 May 1988. Newsbank SOC file 53: E9.

Smith, Dennis A. "The Gospel According to the United States: Evangelical Broadcasting in Central America." *American Evangelicals and the Mass Media*. Ed. Quentin J. Schultze. Grand Rapids: Academie, 1990.

Stepp, Laura Sessions. "The Swaggart Aftermath." *Washington Post,* 23 February 1988, D1.

Stoll, David. *Is Latin America Turning Protestant?* Berkeley: University of California Press, 1990.

"Swaggart Blasts Roberts for Money Demands." *Presbyterian Journal* 4 February 1987, 63.

"Swaggart Didn't Preach, But He Did Lead the Choir." *Grand Rapids Press*, 11 April 1988, A6.

Swaggart, Jimmy [Lee] and Frances Swaggart. "I Just Want to Say, 'We Love You.' " *The Evangelist,* April 1988, 12.

Swaggart, Jimmy [Lee]. "From Me to You." The Evangelist, May/June 1991, 12.

_____. "God's Priorities." *The Evangelist,* April 1988, 9-10.

_____. Interview. *Good Morning America.* By Steve Fox. ABC. WRTV, Indianapolis. 12 November 1986.

_____. "Our Upcoming Telethon is Our Most Important One Ever." *The Evangelist,* January 1988: 32+.

_____. "A Personal Message." 28 February 1988, letter to supporters of the Jimmy Swaggart Ministries, 1-2.

_____. *Rape of a Nation*. Baton Rouge: Swaggart Ministries, 1985.

_____. *Straight Answers to Tough Questions*. Brentwood: Wolgemuth, 1987.

_____. *To Cross A River*. Baton Rouge: Swaggart Ministries, 1984.

_____. "The Word for Every Day." *The Evangelist* , April 1988, 10.

"Swaggart Reaction Varies." *Colorado Springs Gazette Telegraph*, 27 February 1988. Newsbank SOC file 28: D13.

"Swaggart's Fall: Bad For Business." *Washington Post,* 2 April 1988, C11.

"Swaggart's Wife, Son Ask Viewers for Cash." *Grand Rapids Press*, 16 March 1988, A6.

Toulmin, Stephen, Richard Rieke, and Allan Jaik. *An Introduction to Reasoning*. New York: Macmillan, 1984.

Vatz, Richard E. "The Myth of the Rhetorical Situation." *Philosophy and Rhetoric* 6 (1973): 154-161.

Wall, James M. "Swaggart's Confession: There's Room to Mourn." *Christian Century,* 9 March 1988, 235-236.

Ware, B.L. and Will A. Linkugel. "They Spoke in Defense of Themselves: On the Generic Criticism of Apologia." *Quarterly Journal of Speech* 59 (1973): 273-283.

Warnick, Barbara. "The Narrative Paradigm: Another Story." *Communication Monographs* 56 (March 1989): 39-54.

"We Believe." *The Evangelist*, April 1988, 3.

Wilson, Amy. "Swaggart: The Forgiven." *Ft. Lauderdale Sun-Sentinel*, 12 March 1989, E1.

Witham, Larry, "Swaggart Differs From Other Penitents Only in Celebrity." *Washington Times*, 28 February 1988. Newsbank SOC file 28: B9.

"Why Does the Jimmy Swaggart Telecast Have the Largest Audience in America and the World?" *The Evangelist*, January 1988, 60.

Woodward, Kenneth L. "Swaggart's One-Edged Sword." *Newsweek*, 9 January 1984, 65.

Woodward, Kenneth L. and Mark Miller. "Following Dad to the Pulpit." *Newsweek,* 8 February 1988, 62-63.

"The Word for Every Day." *The Evangelist* April 1988, 10.

Wuthnow, Robert. "Religion and Television: The Public and The Private." *American Evangelicals and the Mass Media*. Ed. Quentin J. Schultze. Grand Rapids: Academie, 1990.

Zarefsky, David. "The Lincoln-Douglas Debates Revisited: The Evolution of Public Argument." *Quarterly Journal of Speech* 72 (1986): 162-184.

Zimmerman, Thomas F. "Priorities and Beliefs of Pentecostals." *Christianity Today,* 4 September 1981, 36.

INDEX

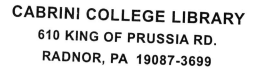